## PRAISE FOR *THE GREENHOUSE APPROACH*

An insightful guide on the underlying roots of innovation thinking and development. *The Greenhouse Approach* reveals what's core and critical to your innovation effectiveness through an intrapreneurial mindset.

— Michele Romanow, serial entrepreneur, co-founder of Clearbanc and SnapSaves, Dragon on CBC's *Dragons' Den*

*The Greenhouse Approach* goes beyond theories of what innovation should look like within organizations. This book questions core ideas that inhibit people and organizations in realizing what innovation can and should be — ideas like the dangers of consensus thinking and applying first principles thinking to how we approach our innovation efforts. An introspective read that is an excellent guide for organizations.

— John Ruffolo, chief executive officer, OMERS Ventures

Chitra Anand addresses the biggest challenge to creativity and innovation: the internal resistance to change and the stubborn or fearful reluctance to consider a new idea or a new process or an entirely new way of doing business. This book should be required reading for all corporate managers.

— Dr. Paula Zobisch, associate professor and program chair, Bachelor of Arts in Entrepreneurship, Forbes School of Business & Technology

*The Greenhouse Approach* takes an enticing look at the concept and importance of intrapreneurship within organizations. Allowing that dynamic to evolve is a critical contribution of value to the enterprise, and essential to growth and sustainability in today's rapidly changing environment.

— Dr. Ray Powers, associate dean and chair of the board of advisors, Forbes School of Business & Technology; director, Knowledge Innovation Center

# THE
# GREENHOUSE
# APPROACH

# THE GREENHOUSE APPROACH

## Cultivating Intrapreneurship in Companies and Organizations

## CHITRA ANAND

### DUNDURN
TORONTO

Cover image: shutterstock.com/VLADGRIN
Printer: Webcom, a division of Marquis Book Printing Inc.

**Library and Archives Canada Cataloguing in Publication**

Anand, Chitra, author
       The greenhouse approach : cultivating intrapreneurship in companies and organizations / Chitra Anand.

Includes bibliographical references and index.
Issued in print and electronic formats.
ISBN 978-1-4597-4285-7 (softcover).--ISBN 978-1-4597-4286-4 (PDF).--
ISBN 978-1-4597-4287-1 (EPUB)

       1. Creative ability in business--Management.  2. Entrepreneurship.
I. Title.

HD53.A53 2019                    658.4'063                    C2018-905753-X
                                                              C2018-905754-8


1   2   3   4   5      23    22    21    20    19

  Canada

We acknowledge the support of the **Canada Council for the Arts**, which last year invested $153 million to bring the arts to Canadians throughout the country, and the **Ontario Arts Council** for our publishing program. We also acknowledge the financial support of the Government of Ontario, through the **Ontario Book Publishing Tax Credit** and **Ontario Creates**, and the **Government of Canada**.

Nous remercions le **Conseil des arts du Canada** de son soutien. L'an dernier, le Conseil a investi 153 millions de dollars pour mettre de l'art dans la vie des Canadiennes et des Canadiens de tout le pays.

Care has been taken to trace the ownership of copyright material used in this book. The author and the publisher welcome any information enabling them to rectify any references or credits in subsequent editions.

— *J. Kirk Howard, President*

The publisher is not responsible for websites or their content unless they are owned by the publisher.

Printed and bound in Canada.

VISIT US AT

dundurn.com  |   @dundurnpress  |   dundurnpress  |   dundurnpress

Dundurn
3 Church Street, Suite 500
Toronto, Ontario, Canada
M5E 1M2

For all the dreamers and doers.

For my children, who constantly remind me
that to be curious is a natural and wondrous state.

For my husband, who has challenged my
mindset daily to evolve my thinking.

For my parents, who taught me that anything
can be achieved through hard work.

Strength does not come from physical capacity ...
it comes from indomitable will.

— Mahatma Gandhi

# CONTENTS

# INTRODUCTION

## Re-imagining Corporations Through Intrapreneurship

IT'S EVERYWHERE. You can't take a breath without being affected by it. *Innovation.*

It quite literally is the air we breathe, and not just in business. Ours is a "blink and you'll miss it" nanosecond global culture. In the time it takes you to read this brief introduction, some aspect of your life will have been changed by innovation.

"Move fast and break things," writes Facebook co-founder and CEO Mark Zuckerberg. "Unless you are breaking some stuff you are not moving fast enough."

But here is the bizarre reality: Many businesses *stifle* innovation. It's true. Innovation sounds great when it comes from the likes of a Zuckerberg or Apple Inc. CEO Tim Cook, but for a surprisingly large number of companies the status quo is mostly what happens. An *aversion to change* business culture is not the product of a lack of the resources necessary to accomplish rejuvenation; in fact, small start-ups are often more successful innovators than mega-corporations. The inability — the unwillingness — to adapt and to change is the consequence of business culture inertia, of a corporate mindset that focuses disproportionately on established organizational structures and processes. Large companies have the resources to effect change, but many of them lack the corporate culture to make meaningful changes.

The question for any business leader or manager in today's global business setting is: *Why?* The argument that runs throughout *The Greenhouse Approach* is that a company that refuses to come to grips with the "why" question — one that cannot adapt to a more flexible approach — faces extinction. It's called a "mindset" for a reason, right? We run into it every single day: wall after wall after wall; layer upon layer upon layer. Does that sound like what companies such as Google or Apple are doing? Well, if these companies are doing it differently, why aren't you and your company? Once that question is answered it becomes possible to make the alterations necessary to change the corporate mindset, the company's structure and procedures, to unleash the power of innovation.

In our nanosecond culture, consumers and businesses expect more, faster. New technologies and products are hitting the market around the clock, and that means virtually everything you are invested in is essentially obsolete the minute it becomes operational. Think about that for a minute. Likewise, fashions and styles come and go at an ever-accelerating rate. It is hardly a surprise that companies are struggling to maintain relevance in a marketplace that seems to be shifting continually under its feet — especially businesses that cater to consumer *impatience*. Large companies — because of their size and complexity — are particularly vulnerable in a market that moves increasingly to the short- versus the long-term; the hundred-yard dash versus the marathon. New products and services represent significant investments not only in research and development but in time. That's a huge problem; consumers aren't willing to wait. If an "innovation" is unveiled too late, it's likely that it will have already become obsolete or unfashionable. The marketplace has moved on.

The pressure on companies to adapt — and adapt quickly — has increased dramatically, mostly because of three developments: globalization, increased competition, and rise of social media. The upshot is that consumers have unparalleled power over the fate of your business. In the "good old days" corporations had all the power; they dictated what happened in the marketplace. Today, the power is at the fingertips of the consumer.

Globalization has been a game-changer. New developments in technology have made the process of globalization much easier. Companies can do business anywhere. Transactions can happen online with the click of a mouse. Of course, the problem with finding ways to lower or eliminate borders is that what used to be "outside" can now easily migrate "inside." Meaning, while a regional company accustomed to monopolizing a market can benefit from broadening its position in that market, it also finds itself facing unexpected — and often unexpectedly aggressive — new competition from outside. A small but successful feed grain wholesaler in Peoria, Iowa, for instance, may suddenly find itself competing with wholesalers in India or China. Who saw that coming?

Local businesses are not just competing with local businesses anymore. Globalization means your competitor is everywhere and they are probably innovating all the time. The consumer who is not happy with the product or service offered by your company most likely has several alternatives — any or all of which might be preferable to your company! The half-life on consumer loyalty shrinks by the hour. The company that might have taken you or your partners a lifetime to build can be shuttered by the end of the week.

*Where did everybody go?*

Trust me, it can happen just that fast.

Businesses not only need to respond better to increased competition in an increasingly globalized economy, but they must also learn to respond to — and even anticipate — the shifting and evolving needs and preferences of their customers. Get it wrong and you set yourself up for harsh criticism and even viral-style consumer mutinies. The doubled-edged sword of the global marketplace is that the same technology allowing businesses to market their products and services all over the world also encourages consumers to *instantly* communicate their experiences and opinions — good or bad — *around the world.* Simply stated: the internet has given a voice to consumers.

Instant feedback is not necessarily a bad thing. Smart companies are learning to use the net and social media to monitor consumer mood, improve their businesses, and gain sales. We have seen many companies embrace social media, so much so that they have used these platforms to connect with their customers in real time, taking customer service concerns, getting feedback on products and services, and using these platforms to communicate, too.

So, what is a company supposed to do?

\* \* \*

"Innovation" is an overused term and its meaning is frequently misunderstood. Innovation doesn't just result in the creation of a new product or service to market. It can result in the creation of a new billing system to better support your customers, for instance; it could be a new talent acquisition method to better attract and maintain talent, or it could be an improved marketing data system to better understand your customers. These are all ways of being innovative. Innovation is as much a way of thinking as it is the thing achieved.

Okay, that makes innovation sound easy. It isn't. In fact, it's about the hardest thing for any company to adopt. Think about it. Most businesses are highly and heavily structured. Innovation requires a complete rethink of what it means to structure a company culture. The irony is that while the markets globalize and innovate, a majority of companies cling desperately to the old Balkanized models and familiar structures.

For instance, most companies — large companies, especially — have highly structured systems in place when it comes to decision-making. Complex organizational structures and supply chains require not only smart decisions but timely decision-making in order to bring new products and services to the market rapidly. When companies grow, however, the risk is that they become slower — slower to move on ideas, slower to make decisions, and slower to execute them. Innovations that need to be implemented can become mired in a web of processes and procedures. Ultimately, great ideas get lost.

How can you solve this problem? I believe the solution lies in building a culture of *intrapreneurship*.

What is an intrapreneur? An intrapreneur is someone who applies an entrepreneurial approach within a large company. Intrapreneurs challenge conventional thinking in order to drive creativity, innovation, and new ways of approaching business. The people within your companies who are intrapreneurial are more important now than ever before. These people are the mavericks, the disruptors, the trendspotters, the researchers, and the connectors. These are the people who know how to navigate companies to implement projects and ideas quickly and flawlessly; they are the ones who can see patterns and themes in your business; they are the ones who help execute quickly.

It is the intrapreneurs within your companies that will generate the great ideas needed to solve the company's problems, who will be best at realizing those great ideas.

How do *intrapreneurs* differ from *entrepreneurs*? Simple answer: the former acts from *within* and the latter from *outside* the company. An entrepreneur uses their own capital and resources to build their own business, while an intrapreneur uses those of a company to help make that company more successful. An entrepreneur typically operates independently, while an intrapreneur has dependencies — usually interdepartmental ones — whose help is required in order to move packages of work or information. The entrepreneur is interested mostly in figuring out how to buy the hill and the ball; the intrapreneur is focused more on how a company's talent and resources can be optimized to roll the ball up that hill.

Despite these differences, entrepreneurs and intrapreneurs share a passion for creating new opportunities, developing new products, techniques, or business lines. They are driven to do all that is necessary to complete a project and make it a success.

What are the characteristics, distinct traits, and attributes of an intrapreneur?

- Intrapreneurs are disruptive. They are disruptive because they ask people within the company to see things in a different light, to do things differently. People are not necessarily okay with that.
- Intrapreneurs have a natural ability to spot trends and see things before they happen. Intrapreneurs are constantly researching, observing, and reading.
- Intrapreneurs cultivate ideas. They are not necessarily only idea people, but if given an idea, they will cultivate it, nurturing that seed until the idea flourishes, emerging as a complete, fully drawn-out plan. Since intrapreneurs know that people may have objections to the idea or plan, they work harder, going three or four steps farther to make sure the plan answers all possible questions, fills all possible gaps.

- Intrapreneurs know how to pivot. They can change directions, and do so without fear, because they have an innate inner confidence and strong intuition that drives them toward the end goal. They are flexible but remain focused, which is important because change is constant in business.
- Intrapreneurs are driven by passion and by what they really believe in. Whether they are focusing on a cause, an idea, or a solution, they are really passionate about it, and when you are passionate about what you are doing, you naturally and organically do your best work.

I have spent my career in the corporate world, working with some of North America's top companies and leaders. It has been an immensely rewarding experience, but it has also been a frustrating experience at times. I am curious by nature, prone to question the status quo, and fascinated with pursuing unexplored paths and hidden byways for better ways of doing and thinking about things. It's a way of thinking that seems natural and normal to me, and, what I will assert throughout *The Greenhouse Approach*, is that the same is true for you. The problem is, the conventional "corporate mindset" virtually all of us come up against thinks it isn't!

Intrapreneurship is the gateway to a fresh-thinking approach to how companies can operate more efficiently and profitably and in a more sustainable way in our hyper-competitive economic culture; it is an open door to unleashing creative thinking, encouraging experimentation, and managing productive risk-taking, all of which will ultimately drive innovative thinking *from within*.

\* \* \*

Once upon a time Abercrombie & Fitch was the "coolest" retailer; it was all the rage among teenagers and young adults. The company started out as a luxury sporting and excursion goods brand, then shifted its focus to target the eighteen- to twenty-two-year-old group who aspired to wear popular "casual luxury" clothing. The company succeeded immensely and created three offshoot brands. With all that success, however, it wasn't long before warning signs appeared. Smaller and aggressive entrants invaded Abercrombie's domain and threatened market share. Also, the habits and behaviours of its customers were changing faster than the company was used to, and instead of being the trendsetters, the company was surrendering consumer choices to upstarts like Zara and H&M, hip newcomers with a different look and feel who were connecting directly to the preferences of young consumers.

Instead of maintaining a steady growth and profit trajectory, sales started flattening and before long the arrow was turning downward. The company had lost its way.

In addition, increasing numbers of customers were enthusiastic about patronizing companies that were on the "socially responsible" spectrum. Phrases like "diversity" and "fair trade" hit advertising and marketing copy. Not long ago it was enough to know what a company produced; just as important was how and where and at what cost. Abercrombie lost ground, as well, to outlets that competed with the company via deep discounts from online sales — a domain that up to that point had been as foreign to them as the surface of Mars. "Who the heck wants to shop online when they can visit one of our stores?"

Well . . .

An important thing to remember about Abercrombie & Fitch is that the company was being run by extremely bright and experienced professionals who were *supposed to know* what they were doing. What happened? The more interesting question for us is, why does it happen so often? BlackBerry, Blockbuster Video, Tower Records, Sears, Kodak — the list goes on.

*The Greenhouse Approach* is a manifesto to help your company thrive in today's highly competitive marketplace. Innovation cannot be accidental or the consequence of an afterthought; it must be embedded in the company's DNA. It isn't a "now and then" approach but a 24/7 way of thinking that permeates and motivates behaviour across the entire company — from boardroom to mailroom.

In my professional experience, I have seen companies — too many companies, frankly — that feature "innovation incubators" that operate in a silo. Of course there should be an area of the business dedicated to research and development; success in business depends on the fostering of innovation and creativity throughout the company. But creating a silo of innovation is like investing in an expensive landscaping project and only watering a tiny section of the garden. Intrapreneurial culture must be fostered everywhere. A deliberate and intentional way of behaving is needed, a way of being, a way of thinking, a culture or movement. Businesses must be nimble, building an environment where it is safe to take risks by experimenting, failing, and learning. Businesses must hire and support *innovative disruptors* to work within their companies, effectively creating a culture of experimentation. A culture of curiosity. A culture of intrapreneurship.

I believe that not only is intrapreneurship the best approach to business management, but, in order for today's large companies to survive and thrive, there must be a deliberate and intentional entrepreneurial movement from within. Intrapreneurship needs to be the new way of thinking and operating in order for companies to survive.

It might seem like a huge risk. It might seem safer to adopt a "wait and see" approach. But the biggest risk you and your company face is the consequences of complacency.

* * *

Blink and you might miss it.

What is *it*? Innovative thinking that will carry your company successfully into the future. After years of studying the corporate world from the inside out, I came up with the concept of a "greenhouse" as a practical analogy for how companies can foster innovative thinking. As we all know, a greenhouse provides an environment that encourages plants to flourish. Properly run, companies can emulate greenhouses, providing an environment that fosters the innovation necessary for success. *The Greenhouse Approach* shows how this can be done.

The first part of the book examines the psychology of businesses and human beings. It looks at certain foundational ideas of what is normal and desirable, and examines how these ideas manifest themselves in our work lives and ultimately within companies. These ideas condition and limit our thinking, but if we can change the way that we think, it is possible to make better decisions, decisions that will ultimately unleash creativity and innovation. This shift in mindset is fundamental if intrapreneurial thinking is to flourish.

There are four main areas in which change is needed.

## RULES

The first change involves rules and the role that rules play in our ability to think creatively. Don't get me wrong. I am not an anarchist. We all need rules. Life couldn't operate without them. Remember as a kid, however, when you asked your parents "how come?" and they answered "because I said so"? Was that a satisfactory answer? *Of course not.* It frustrated you! That is what I mean. A rule can act as a euphemism for conventional behaviour and practices. Think of rules as the strict, inflexible, and *accepted* norms that exist in most companies and that tend to regulate, shape, and structure our thinking about the jobs we do and how we do them, about our goals, our workplace interactions, our expectations, and so on. Too many rules suppress creative (disruptive) thinking and undermine the risk-taking that a healthy company needs to thrive.

## CONSENSUS

Just as rules are limiting in a company, so, too, is the need for consensus in decision-making. For most of our lives, we have been conditioned to think that the majority rules. With elections and surveys, the majority decides what choices are made. The same is true in business. I recall many times sitting around a boardroom table, discussing the need for a decision, and spending precious time trying to get majority agreement. I have always questioned this approach. Generally, compelling compliance does not encourage innovation.

Broad agreement may minimize the potential for conflict regarding a decision, but that doesn't mean that the decision is a good one. Conflict often is necessary to purge the brain — and the boardroom — of cobwebbed thinking and can promote instead the innovation that actually reveals the best decision. Without friction there is no spark, right? So, eliminating friction, striving for majority agreement, is a sure way to inhibit the creative spark so necessary for innovation. An interesting experiment is to think of the process less as a majority versus a minority — a winner and a loser — than as two rival but *non-competitive* perspectives. There is no such thing as a winner when it comes to perspective. And what is more important in the long run? Being with the majority or learning how to view a problem from several perspectives and following the one that fulfills your company's vision?

## CURIOSITY

Curiosity is one of the most important characteristics necessary for success; in fact, Microsoft CEO Bill Gates insists it is one of the top traits that he looks for in people when seeking talent. We are born naturally curious, but somewhere along the way we lose it. Why? Curiosity is a form of disruption that by its nature challenges the accepted and the orthodox. Companies might like to pretend they value curiosity from their workforce, but chances are they don't. Bill Gates does, and you can see the results. So do executives like Tim Cook and Mark Zuckerberg. It isn't just "good copy" for them.

The challenge for you as a "greenhousing" company is to reignite the curiosity that is natural to us as human beings and channel that creative disruption into a powerful and self-sustaining current of innovation.

## ASSUMPTIONS

We make assumptions every day. We all make decisions and judgments *based* on those assumptions. How often, however, do we stop to examine the truth of those assumptions? If you are like most people, hardly ever. So we need to rewire our brains. We need to subject our assumptions to rigorous examination. Is the assumption one that warrants our attention, or is it — as it often is — merely the product or consequence of conventional or historic behaviour that has you asking why it's done this way? What I have learned from my many years' experience in the corporate trenches is that examining our assumptions — to be willing to bend enough to incorporate alternative assumptions — can be a very difficult but rewarding exercise. It is, however, fundamental to the greenhouse approach.

\* \* \*

In Part Two of the book we focus on a collection of guiding principles necessary for companies to thrive into the future. Part Three presents a practical application of the model. The case study shows how the four phases of the model can be applied. This section brings the guiding principles to life, helping to clarify how all of the ideas can come together in a meaningful way.

Throughout *The Greenhouse Approach* you will hear from many of the most successful and most sought-out leaders and thinkers in the business world about the importance of innovation. My hope is that reading *The Greenhouse Approach* will inspire you to think differently and shift your preconceived ideas. As much as this book is about innovation and how to really inspire a culture of intrapreneurship, it is also about the psychology of business. It makes you think, I hope, about why and how we do the things we do.

If there is one thing that we all need to realize, it is this: business is about behaviours and thinking. We need to identify and cultivate the types of behaviours needed in order for businesses to flourish.

In writing *The Greenhouse Approach*, I had one question in mind: Can companies create a culture of intrapreneurship by changing how they cultivate their people, problem-solve, and think about their own leadership styles?

After reading this book, you will be able to

- re-imagine rules, and how rules can inhibit creative thinking. To reassess them within your company to unleash true innovation.
- rethink how you make decisions as a business professional. Question the importance we put on consensus thinking.
- learn to embrace conflict. Conflict is good when it comes to pushing boundaries and developing new ideas.

- appreciate different perspectives. Acknowledge that the need to be right is limiting, particularly around innovation. Let the overarching goals of the project and company be your North Star.
- reignite your curious self and other inquisitive people within your company. Understand how to appreciate and better support them.
- understand how the role of problem solving can be applied within your company. Take the four phases of the problem-solving methodology and apply them in some of the challenges that you have within your company.

*The Greenhouse Approach* is not "pie in the sky" economic or management theory; it is a down-to-earth guide showing you how you can make your company or business intentional, mindful, and deliberate. Businesses must be intentional about putting intrapreneurship into practice, mobilizing the truly inspired people within their workforce by challenging, supporting, nurturing, accommodating, and rewarding intrapreneurial behaviour.

If you think your company may be too small (or too large) to incorporate the greenhouse approach, I implore you to think again. Businesses of any size in virtually any sector can make the decision to shift to a model of intrapreneurship.

*The Greenhouse Approach* shows how companies and businesses can change their cultures, strategies, and ways of "thinking and doing" to gain a more engaged and empowered workforce of innovators. I know it works because I have seen it applied.

Are you ready to innovate?

PART ONE

# CHANGING THE STATUS QUO

# CHAPTER ONE

## Growth Mindsets

HOW CAN YOU and your company develop and foster intrapreneurship?

The first thing that needs to change is what we call the "core mindset." It's necessary to abandon old ways of thinking — the fixed and inflexible mindset — and to encourage instead a *growth mindset*. The ideas of intrapreneurship and growth mindset complement each other. So, what is a growth mindset?

The concepts of a fixed versus a growth mindset originated in the work of Stanford psychologist Carol Dweck and were synthesized in her remarkably insightful *Mindset: The New Psychology of Success* — an inquiry into the power of our beliefs, both conscious and unconscious, and how changing even the simplest of them can have profound impacts on nearly every aspect of our lives.

A fixed mindset assumes that our character, intelligence, and creative ability are static and that we can't alter them in any meaningful way. A growth mindset, on the other hand, thrives on challenges as opportunities for growth. For instance, it embraces failure as a welcome learning opportunity — a springboard for stretching and enhancing our abilities. If as children we had never risked falling off our bikes, we never would have mastered the skills required, right? Why should business be any different?

Research tells us that employees who have a growth mindset and an overall openness about what they do report feeling far more empowered and committed.\* Of course, such a mindset cannot flourish in an environment that does not support and reward it. A growth mindset must be part of a company's DNA. Companies, in order to flourish, must provide the necessary organizational support for collaboration and innovation.

And that is where intrapreneurship comes in. As noted above, intrapreneurship and a growth mindset are complementary; in order to build and develop a culture of intrapreneurship, a growth mindset is essential.

Sara Briggs, managing editor of InformED, lists the ways to develop a growth mindset on her website (opencolleges.edu.au/informed/features/develop-a-growth-mindset).

## TWENTY-FIVE WAYS TO DEVELOP A GROWTH MINDSET

1. **Acknowledge and embrace imperfections.** Hiding from your weaknesses means you'll never overcome them.
2. **View challenges as opportunities.** Having a growth mindset means relishing opportunities for self-improvement. Learn more about how to fail well.
3. **Try different learning tactics.** There's no one-size-fits-all model for learning. What works for one person may not work for you. Learn about learning strategies.
4. **Follow the research on brain plasticity.** The brain isn't fixed; the mind shouldn't be either.
5. **Replace the word "failing" with the word "learning."** When you make a mistake or fall short of a goal, you haven't failed; you've learned.
6. **Stop seeking approval.** When you prioritize approval over learning, you sacrifice your own potential for growth.
7. **Value the process over the end result.** Intelligent people enjoy the learning process, and don't mind when it continues beyond an expected time frame.
8. **Cultivate a sense of purpose.** Dweck's research also showed that students with a growth mindset had a greater sense of purpose. Keep the big picture in mind.

---

\* Senn Delaney, "Why Fostering a Growth Mindset in Organizations Matters" (Senn Delaney, 2014), http://knowledge.senndelaney.com/docs/thought_papers/pdf/stanford_agilitystudy_hart.pdf.

9. **Celebrate growth with others.** If you truly appreciate growth, you'll want to share your progress with others.

10. **Emphasize growth over speed.** Learning fast isn't the same as learning well, and learning well sometimes requires allowing time for mistakes.

11. **Reward actions, not traits.** Tell students when they're doing something smart, not just being smart.

12. **Redefine "genius."** The myth's been busted; genius requires hard work, not talent alone.

13. **Portray criticism as positive.** You don't have to use that hackneyed term, "constructive criticism," but you do have to believe in the concept.

14. **Disassociate improvement from failure.** Stop assuming that "room for improvement" translates into failure.

15. **Provide regular opportunities for reflection.** Let students reflect on their learning at least once a day.

16. **Place effort before talent.** Hard work should always be rewarded before inherent skill.

17. **Highlight the relationship between learning and "brain training."** The brain is like a muscle that needs to be worked out, just like the body.

18. **Cultivate grit.** Students with that extra bit of determination will be more likely to seek approval from themselves rather than others.

19. **Abandon the image.** "Naturally smart" sounds just about as believable as "spontaneous generation." You won't achieve the image if you're not ready for the work.

20. **Use the word "yet."** Dweck says "not yet" has become one of her favourite phrases. Whenever you see students struggling with a task, tell them they haven't mastered it yet.

21. **Learn from other people's mistakes.** It's not always wise to compare yourself to others, but it is important to realize that humans share the same weaknesses.

22. **Make a new goal for every goal accomplished.** You'll never be done learning. Just because your midterm exam is over doesn't mean you should stop being interested in a subject. Growth-minded people know how to constantly create new goals to keep themselves stimulated.

23. **Take risks in the company of others.** Stop trying to save face all the time and just let yourself goof up now and then. It will make it easier to take risks in the future.
24. **Think realistically about time and effort.** It takes time to learn. Don't expect to master every topic under the sun in one sitting.
25. **Take ownership over your attitude.** Once you develop a growth mindset, own it. Acknowledge yourself as someone who possesses a growth mentality and be proud to let it guide you throughout your educational career.

A growth mindset requires an openness to rethink and re-examine. As a business leader you know how frustrating it is when a static mindset prevails within a company. Instead of coming to their jobs excited and energized by the opportunities to have meaningful interactions, too many employees walk around with dead eyes and listless attitudes — more like robots than human beings. Yes, we all need to purge the cobwebs; we need to re-examine and re-think. Perhaps the most important requirement, however, is the willingness to change. A culture will not evolve on its own; it has to be made to evolve. How does that happen? If you want a sunny day, don't walk around with an open umbrella!

In my extensive study of corporations over many years, I have discovered a common set of ideas and practices that need to be re-thought and changed. Below are the main ones.

## RULES, PROCESSES, AND PROCEDURES

What role do rules, processes, and procedures play when trying to drive creative thinking and experimentation? How do they hinder the creative process even before it starts?

## DECISION-MAKING

Within every company decisions need to be made every day. Decision-making is perhaps the most misunderstood area of management, and considering how critical it is to sound business operation, it is amazing how much we overestimate our own good decision-making skills. Whether it's business or life, we all need a compass; we need a North Star as a reliable means for orienting our behaviour and decision-making. Pushing for a consensus, for instance, can actually distract us from the straight and the true. The goal is not consensus; the goal is your North Star.

## CURIOSITY

"The first and the simplest emotion which we discover in the human mind," observed the great philosopher and politician Edmund Burke, "is curiosity."

Curiosity is a feature of human intuition we are all born with, but somewhere down the line it is lost. By the time we reach adulthood, it is all but gone, and so very little is carried with us into the workforce. While many companies insist they want and value curiousity, the question really is ... do they? A curious person will challenge the status quo. A curious person will upset the apple cart with potentially risky or embarrassing questions about how and why things are done the way they are. Are you *sure* you are prepared for that kind — that level — of confrontation? It has been my experience that most company managers and executives aren't. It isn't a mindset they are used to or comfortable with. Ask yourself, is your boardroom more often a bored room?

Remember, innovation rarely arrives ahead of schedule wrapped up with a bow.

## FIRST PRINCIPLES

What role do first principles play when we make decisions that will ultimately impact the directions we take?

We addressed briefly in the introduction the problem with assumptions. We need them, but we don't need *all of* them. Basically, first principles are the fundamentals without which a company cannot survive as *the* company. Think of it as you might when meeting a friend who seems a bit off. What do we say? "You don't seem yourself today." Business is the same. First principles define who you are as a company and what your vision is. It's the core beliefs from which all other behaviour and decision-making evolves. First principles are your North Star. First principles do not change.

Assumptions, on the other hand, might be the outdated and outmoded and conventional ways of thinking that prevent your company from thriving. Assumptions can be jettisoned; first principles need to be routinely reinforced.

\* \* \*

Once we can open our minds to these new foundational ways of thinking, we are well on our way to unleashing the power of innovation from within. Now, let's begin with rules.

# CHAPTER TWO

## Planting the Seeds of Rebellion

There's a rebel lying deep in my soul.

— Clint Eastwood

**IN ORDER TO HAVE** *true* innovation — to really break through and to disrupt and see things in a radically different light — rules must be broken.

My guess is right now you might be inclined to toss this book defiantly across the room in disbelief. "We need to break rules? What kind of crazy advice is that? It will be chaos!"

Remember what we said about rules. It's basically the same with first principles versus assumptions: we need both, but we need *much more* of one and *much less* of the other. What I want to do in this chapter is urge you to rethink the way you and your company do things; I want you to challenge your own assumptions. I want you to be your own rebel; I want you to be your own disruptor.

Of course, if you are like most people, your first response will be resistance. A simple fact is that we tend to be okay with the status quo. And we will accommodate the status quo as long as we can. When we were children at school there was always at least one kid who refused to behave. "You're making it difficult for all the other children!" warned the teacher. Here's the thing: for whatever reason, that kid *saw* the world differently. They also saw their own role in the world differently. They didn't care about obeying the rules or complying with an agenda. Isn't that why we call them "rebels"?

Here's a question that underscores everything that we will be discussing, not only in this chapter but throughout *The Greeenhouse Approach*: When it comes to breaking rules, who wins and who loses? Another perspective on this question might be thinking about the difference between a rebellion and a mutiny. Here's a hint: one can be led and directed, the other can't.

\* \* \*

Salt.

It's a simple commodity known (and readily available) to us all. We sprinkle it on foods to bring out their flavours. Some of us use salt to preserve foods, and many of us try not to eat too much of it.

For most people today, that's where the salt connection ends.

But salt is symbolic to Indians. It is a symbol of freedom and independence.

Salt was once a highly valued substance. Roman soldiers were sometimes paid in salt rather than gold. (He wasn't worth his salt.) The word "salary" comes from the Latin word for "salt."

During the nineteenth century, India was under the British Raj (British Rule), and Indian nationals were severely oppressed. The primary objective of the Raj? To export cheap raw materials from India to England. To do this, the Raj imposed unfair laws on the native Indian population, many of whom were treated cruelly, imprisoned, and died of starvation.

To prevent salt smuggling and to collect customs on tobacco, sugar, and other commodities, the Raj constructed a four-thousand-kilometre wall basically down the centre of the county. Known as the "Inland Customs Line," the wall was three metres high and four metres thick. It was constructed from materials like thorny bushes, stakes, and prickly plum branches and was designed to be impenetrable.

For the enslaved Indians, this wall was a visible and humiliating symbol of the oppression of the British Raj. It stood for ten years, until 1879, when it was decided it posed too great a barrier to travel and trade; maintenance costs, too, proved exorbitantly high.

The removal of the wall, however, failed to address the core problem of the oppression of India's enormous population. Indians were prevented from collecting or selling salt, for instance, a staple in the Indian diet. The Salt Act of 1882 required Indians to buy salt only from the British (and, of course, the commodity was heavily taxed, preventing most citizens from being able to afford it).

Okay. What does any of this have to do with business and innovation?

## GANDHI: THE REBEL OF PASSIVE RESISTANCE

Mahatma Gandhi was a great man. He was the leader of the independence movement that liberated India from British rule. Most astonishingly, he achieved this through non-violent means, encouraging acts of mass civil disobedience.

One of the most famous examples of these was the Salt March.

In 1930, Mahatma Gandhi made a bold statement that would lead to the liberation of India. His Salt March saw him (and tens of thousands of followers) march 240 kilometres to the ocean. The goal was to simply pick up a handful of salt in defiance of the Salt Act.

Gandhi and sixty thousand others were arrested in this peaceful protest, but Gandhi was a force to be reckoned with. The mass civil disobedience led by Gandhi continued after his imprisonment and it continued until he and the viceroy of India were able to come to an agreement that would see Gandhi travel to London to be given a voice at a conference on the future of India. Gandhi was acknowledged by the British as a force it could neither ignore nor overwhelm. Gandhi's strategy of peaceful resistance changed history, and he would become an inspiration for other human rights leaders like Martin Luther King, Jr. and Nelson Mandela.

Their struggles are an incredibly powerful lesson in how commitment to first principles, and thinking differently about the power of the status quo can be liberating. An adversary is never so powerful as to be invincible — especially when the adversary is no farther away than our own assumptions or habits. The key is being a creative disruptor. Like Coco Chanel.

## CHANEL

Following the death of her mother, twelve-year-old Gabrielle Bonheur Chanel was placed in an orphanage. The nuns who raised her taught her to sew, a skill that would benefit the girl later in life.

You may know Gabrielle Chanel better by her nickname, Coco — a woman who dared to be different.

A rebel in the world of fashion, Chanel was the first designer to insist that women's fashions could be comfortable and stylish at the same time. She loosened waistlines, shortened skirts, and encouraged women to do away with corsets. She borrowed inspiration from menswear and introduced the world to the Chanel suit, with its classic well-fitted skirt and collarless jacket. She took the colour black, a colour that had always been reserved for mourning, and brought us the iconic little black dress, the ultimate symbol of chic, and still a staple in every woman's closet.

Coco Chanel was anything but conventional, and she built a formidable career that would allow her to fearlessly break the rules. She expressed her rebellion through her passion for design.

## RULES WERE MADE TO BE BROKEN

Rules, according to *Webster's Dictionary*, are "a set of explicit or understood regulations or principles governing conduct within a particular activity or sphere."

Okay, those kind of rules seem fine.

Society, people, and companies need some kind of governing principles to help guide them so that they act in a sensible way.

A few questions follow, though. What are the rules? Who sets them? And how do those who set the rules use them? According to the *Oxford Dictionary of English*, to rule is to "exercise ultimate power or authority over an area and its people," or to have "a feeling of having a powerful and restricting influence on a person's life"

So, to rule is to have power. As we all know, power can be used to help or to hurt, to create or destroy. This is true in the world at large and it is true in companies. Management has the power to set the rules, and those rules can help to foster creativity and intrapreneurship or they can hinder them. The rules can set people free to create and be truly innovative, or they can serve as a means of control, instilling a sense of fear, to solidify the dominance of those who set the rules. If the rules don't encourage freedom, risk-taking, and creativity, if employees are forced to work in an atmosphere of fear, dominated and controlled by supervisors hovering over them, how can a change mindset and intrapreneurship flourish?

The answer is simple: it cannot and will not.

I interviewed the CEO of a creative agency, who said, "Processes within companies are hindrances for innovation, thus we need to change the way they are used. We need to shift our mindset and think about exploring the art of the possible. When you start to explore this, failure will happen, which is not a bad thing. We need to think about things differently."

So let's do that. Let's think about rules in a broader context for a moment.

If you think back to your childhood, you'll recall that the rules you lived under likely had a very explicit function. Most things we did as kids were based around the idea of cause and consequence. Causality (also referred to as causation) is the relationship between an event (the *cause*) and a second event (the *effect*), where the first event is understood to be responsible for the second. As kids we were taught this and this is how we've grown to understand the way rules work. Of course, parents must set rules for children to help govern their behaviour, but they must also allow them the freedom to help them develop their own belief systems. The rules we learned and the belief systems we developed are what drive our behaviour. We go through life understanding cause and effect. We do what we're supposed to do or we suffer a consequence.

Dr. Amanda Beaman is a clinical psychologist and an expert in cognitive behaviour. She focuses largely on the study of mental processes, perception, problem solving, creativity, and reasoning. When she starts working with a new patient, she says, before doing anything else, she seeks to identify the core beliefs that might be directing that person's behaviour. According to Dr. Beaman our core beliefs shape us and everything we do. They drive our decisions and influence the way we look at the world. As children, we were told that in order to play outside, our homework must be done first. That if we wanted to go to a friend's house, we had to finish our chores; if we don't do what we're supposed to do, there will be a negative consequence. It's how we're brought up — cause and effect. If we don't follow the rules, we lose a privilege. This belief system is then carried with us throughout our adult lives and, for the most part, it is how we govern ourselves.

At the heart of all of this is fear: the fear of breaking rules, for instance, and the consequences that will come as a result of doing so. Fear of punishment has extremely negative effects in the personal lives of people. The same is true in companies. Nothing kills workplace culture and innovation faster than fear. Fear prevents employees from asking questions, from speaking up and being disruptive. Fear prevents truths from emerging.

Instead of punishing people for breaking rules, imagine what might happen if employees were not scared — if people felt safe to push the limits. What if we re-imagined the rules and the consequences of breaking rules that make people afraid? Imagine the type of innovation that we might see as a result.

## RULES IN BUSINESS

Policies and procedures exist within companies primarily to ensure the rules are followed. Rules are not necessarily barriers to innovation, remember. Overuse or an overly zealous and inflexible enforcement of rules, however, can be. Problems can arise when a company fails to keep perspective, focuses too closely on policies, and loses sight of the goal — the work itself. As a result, people spend too much time asking for permission, obtaining approval, filling out forms, attending unnecessary meetings, and writing irrelevant emails.

Processes should simplify things, and when they're smart, they do. Without well-thought-out processes in place, companies would have a difficult time functioning and being productive. The problem occurs when there are too many processes in place, when they are too rigid, and when they are so complex that completing all the tasks involved with fulfilling them is overwhelming. Employees spend so much of their time with busy work that there is little time to be creative. With calendars filled with "priority" tasks, the work you want your employees to be doing keeps getting pushed aside, and innovation takes a backseat. People lose their passion and creativity when they are stifled by procedures and processes.

Many times I've been in a meeting and the team was asked to come up with a concept or campaign idea. The hope is that everyone will be energized to contribute as many great ideas as possible, but that is rare — especially in most conventional business environments. Unless brainstorming is habitual — par to the company's DNA — team members' instincts are to resist airing ideas until others have done so first. I call it "testing the waters." But let's say halfway through the meeting a big idea lands on the table. What happens next?

The roadblocks start appearing. "It will be too hard to get approved," or "It will take forever to get funding," or, "It will be too hard to get past legal."

You may have noticed in your own experiences that we find it much easier to articulate the negative than the positive. Ask a friend why she hates a movie she just saw and chances are she can be very specific. If she liked it, however, she might shrug and conclude with something ambiguous. "I don't know really. I just really liked it." Second — and more importantly — criticism often has less to do with the idea and its potential than conventional objections about *implementation*: funding, approval, legal, and so on.

None of these factors, however, have anything to do with the value and validity of the original idea. Think about it: the most obvious feature of a new and innovative idea is that it won't fit neatly into the structure of the status quo. It's exactly why it is an innovation! Not only do you need new ideas, you and your company need to understand how to accept new ideas — how to think innovatively about what is being innovated.

It's a scenario played out all too often, and the consequences of the debilitating inertia and loss of morale that result can be disastrous. Yes, practical considerations need to be kept in mind, and, yes, caution is needed, but so too is risk-taking. I am not saying that we don't need rules, processes, or governance. What I am saying is that we need them to be flexible, with leaders paving the way for creators to create.

Blue-sky thinking, creative ideas not limited by current thinking or beliefs, needs to be encouraged. If you want blue-sky thinking, you can't confine your people by rules and processes.

With blue-sky thinking, you start with the mindset of "What if?"

If you ask "What if?" your mind is automatically freed. You can let your imagination wander, free of constraints. You are empowered to look at potential and explore new possibilities.

This is how you get real ideas. That is how people start thinking creatively.

A critical function of any successful manager or team leader is to remove the boundaries that restrain and restrict the team's thinking. Don't get so caught up in process that you lose your vision. Remember that your role as a leader is to infuse and reinforce the power of creativity. When your team is imagining new possibilities, make sure that the rules are not hindering the incubation of creative ideas. Deal with the details and complications later. Don't allow standard practices to control your team's creative thought process.

One of the key traits of a true intrapreneur is the ability to break rules ... systematically. The ability to break rules is an art, particularly within companies. I am not saying do anything that is illegal or against corporate policy, but if you push boundaries, the result can be meaningful innovation. Intrapreneurs are excellent at understanding what the rules are. They study them in order to better understand what kind of calculated risks can be assumed and which ones can be challenged when focusing on breakthrough ideas. Intrapreneurs do not stop at organizational boundaries; they bend rules that hinder them from achieving their goals.

If a business or organization wants to leap forward, it needs to rethink the rules it operates under. Do those rules make sense? Should they be altered? What if rules were fluid? What if they were malleable? What outcomes would we see if we re-imagined rules?

Rules should be rethought of as guiding principles that can be negotiated or altered, as needed. Guiding principles are a set of values and belief systems that help guide and navigate you, rather than rules which instill fear and power dynamics. This is where leadership needs to step in.

## PRINCIPLES VERSUS RULES

Our personal principles motivate us to do what we feel are the right things and they prevent us from doing things we believe to be wrong.

Rules force us to do what someone else deems to be right and to not do what they think is wrong. What if we used principles to lead within companies, instead of rules?

When people start to focus on what is good and right or in the best interest of the company, as defined by guiding principles, they will be open to share more ideas, push boundaries, think creatively, and collaborate. Collaboration, in turn, builds trust. And trust tends to defuse reluctance and fear. When everyone feels that he or she is actively engaged with the outcome, obstacles are overcome naturally. This culture of complete company-wide engagement is when the magic happens. Sharing breeds trust and trust breeds ideas and creativity.

\* \* \*

The world is changing. Companies need to be open to rethinking the way things are done in order to adapt, compete, and sustain themselves.

An example.

Driving to work Monday through Friday for a 9-to-5 job is becoming a thing of the past. This traditional work structure and rule of how to work is no longer relevant. It has come to the end of its life. We need to rethink the 9-to-5 rule by developing guidelines and principles on how to work and how to best support our employees, customers, colleagues, and partners in this new world of work by making the best use of our technology.

We are curators of our lives and we have twenty-four hours in a day to use. Technology can help us manage what we need to get done.

For instance, work/life integration is very important, especially for millennials and mothers trying to re-enter the workforce. The lines have blurred as a result of technology, and we will always have a need and desire for work flexibility. I have personally never really experienced balance; I've had integration instead. How I best made use of technology is what worked for my days. As a working mother, if I was required to tend to my children during the day, I needed to do so, and I could easily pick up where I left off, after hours. If I wanted to attend a yoga class at 4:00 p.m., I would do so, and adjust my work hours accordingly.

Companies must be willing to shift to fluidity, and as long as output is there, when it gets done should be irrelevant. Leaders must re-imagine what their office culture looks like.

We are an always-on culture. We check our phones in the morning, again at night, and countless times in between. We aren't working nine to five anymore. Our days start earlier and end later. In between, we have other things to do. We're parents, caregivers to aging parents, some of us have career portfolios where we juggle multiple jobs.

As a mother, I cannot think about my day as nine to five because a lot of important things happen in that window, for my kids. I have to take them to school, I might want to attend some of their classes, and I might have to pick them up when they're sick. Additionally, I might need to leave for an appointment or take one of my parents to the doctor.

This doesn't mean I am not an effective employee. I use technology in a responsible way. If I leave work at two o'clock, I will pick it up later. I can work from wherever and whenever. Bottom line: If business really wants to take advantage of all the talent there is out there, it will need to break its rules. You don't hunt where the prey ain't, right?

The same disruption that is upending where we work is just as relevant when it comes to how we work. Traditional thinking is no longer relevant. Conventional thinking is the real risk factor. It might be the company your grandfather founded, but it's no longer a business climate your grandfather will recognize, so you can't keep employing the same clichéd and hide-bound moth-eaten strategies and practices.

Leadership needs to step in and help the "creatives" articulate their ideas and realize them from incubation to execution.

Forget about rules. Think about principles. Ideally what will happen is that over time the first principles become the new rules. Again, however, this Darwinian evolution of business culture will not happen entirely on its own: you need to create the conditions to make evolution happen. This is the greenhouse approach.

* * *

Raja Rajamannar is chief marketing and communications officer and president of Healthcare Business, Mastercard, and has been listed among *Forbes's* "Top 10 World's Most Influential CMOs," *Business Insider's* "Top 50 Most Innovative CMOs in the World," *Adweek's* "Most Tech-Savvy CMOs," and iMedia's "25 Top Marketing Innovators."

If rules and regulations become fixed, I asked him, if a company is too rigid, does intrapreneurship become stifled? If a new idea has to go through ten processes before it gets approved, haven't you killed the creativity before it ever has a chance?

"If we dismiss people and their ideas," he agreed, "they will lose confidence. If this continues to happen regularly, then we as a company are not about innovation — it is not in our cultural fabric."

Companies need to provide an environment and platform, he said, in which people feel empowered and encouraged to bring these ideas forward and see them come to fruition. If you keep saying "no" and pushing people away, they will stop coming forward. Imagine a child sitting in class, always eagerly raising her hand to answer a question, yet the teacher never calls on her. Day after day, week after week, the pattern continues. Will the child keep raising her hand? No. After being ignored enough times, she will not bother.

The movement from rules to guiding principles may look like this:

- **Develop mutual understanding.** There needs to be a clear definition of the non-negotiables. If you are going to adopt malleable rules, an audit needs to be conducted on what are the foundational rules and processes, and the company needs to set those boundaries. Once those are set, you can communicate that back to the respective teams. They should be able to identify where and how these can be used and applied.

- **Allow people to think for themselves.** Leaders need to let go. Allow people to think and make decisions for themselves. To have an autonomous work environment means to empower your employees to truly decide how work should be completed. This means that managers will need to decrease the amount of approvals needed for a project to be developed and likewise lessen their involvement in the workflow process. Teams should be able to self-govern to some extent. Typically, work gets stuck in approval bottlenecks. Leaders will need to look at this process and determine how they can simplify and minimize it in order to make their teams more accountable and empowered. If you have ten approvals, cut them in half and work around that; see how quickly people will rally to produce great work.

- **Actively remove barriers.** This is the role of leadership. Leaders need to understand that when projects are underway, the creative process needs momentum. In order to keep momentum, leaders need to stay engaged with their teams so that they can be available to move work along should it be halted due to process. Remove roadblocks and be advocates for the work.

- **Rethink processes.** In most companies, the default response when an idea or project is put forward is to organize a meeting to discuss it. There is an overdependence on meetings. People feel the need to have "collective buy-in," they feel that decisions should be "inclusive." These are words that are overused and misunderstood. If the firm's principles are understood and accepted by all, there is no need to continuously consult others about every decision or action. Doing so overwhelms things and results in ideas never getting translated into action because they get stuck in this process. You should audit your processes and see which ones you could eliminate completely. This would boost people's ability to be more productive on the work that they need to get done.

In short, relying on first principles is preferable to relying on rules. Still not convinced? Here's a story someone told me about circus elephants that has stayed with me — I think it's a great analogy for how rules limit us and our potential without us even knowing it.

Although not common now, performing elephants were once a staple of circuses. Those elephants were usually acquired when they were very young. In order to keep these young elephants from escaping, trainers would tie one of the animal's legs to a tree or a pole. The elephant would continuously tug on the rope, trying to get free. Eventually, the elephant learned that it couldn't break free and no longer tugged at the rope. Of course, elephants grow into huge animals, strong enough that one tug on the rope can uproot the tree to which it's tied, but because circus elephants were taught as calves that they couldn't escape, they stopped even bothering to try.

Rules have the ability to limit us, even when our capability is stronger and much more powerful than we think or know.

Restructuring your operation to put forward a set of guiding principles and encouraging your people to push those boundaries will unleash hidden resources of creativity. It will cultivate an environment of innovation and intrapreneurship.

Think of the Coco Chanels and Mahatma Gandhis of the world — the disruptors, the fearless, the mavericks, the visionaries. Those are the types of people you want working for you. And they cannot do their best work if they're bound to rigid rules.

Encourage rebellion, allow rules to shift and change, and then watch those seeds of innovation take root and grow.

# CHAPTER THREE

## Minority Rules

Even if you are a minority of one, the truth is the truth.
— Mahatma Gandhi

THE WORLD IS FLAT. Human flight is not possible. The earth is the centre of the universe. History is replete with examples of when majority thinking was wrong.

Henry Ford said, "If I had asked people what they wanted, they would have said faster horses." The greatest thinkers and leaders in the world have been of the minority: Martin Luther King, Jr., Malala Yousafzai, Nelson Mandela. They were all on the opposite side of the majority. They all believed in something that required change — a cause or a movement, a law, or a societal fix.

We've been taught to believe that the majority rules. But, it is my belief that there is power in minority thinking. Just because someone is in the minority doesn't mean they are wrong. Those who've deviated from the norm have shed light on what the norms should be. The minority has changed the world.

In 2009, Jan Koum co-founded a messaging service called WhatsApp. Koum despised advertising and refused to display ads in his messaging service. He said, "The user experience would always lose, because you had to provide a service to the advertiser. Cellphones are so personal and private to you that putting an advertisement there is not a good experience." Koum was in the minority. People told him that it would never work. Three years later? The service processed ten billion messages daily. By 2013, WhatsApp had four hundred million monthly users and was sold to Facebook for nineteen billion dollars.

Why does the majority still rule? Why is consensus still so important in companies?

* * *

Martin Luther King, Jr., said that "almost always, the creative dedicated minority has made the world a better place."

As children, we are taught to work with one another. We are trained to be obedient and to follow the rules "for our own good." And what is good? Usually what someone else — someone or some entity with more power and authority — has decided is good for us. In other words, we are taught to conform and to be agreeable. Most of us have been conditioned by indoctrination and demands for routinized behaviour for so long that we hardly notice what is happening. We aren't children anymore, but we carry those same conformist imperatives with us into our adult lives and our professional careers.

Again, we aren't advocating on behalf of anarchy or rule-breaking merely for rule-breaking's sake. There has to be a method to the madness. And there is: it's called the greenhouse approach. In fact, I like to tell my skeptical corporate clients that it is really less about "breaking rules" than it is about finding keys to opening doors we don't even realize exist. "Do it this way" and "do it that way" are two doors. How will you know if there is a third or fourth option unless you know what a new door looks like?

## CONFORMITY: SOLOMON ASCH'S CONFORMITY EXPERIMENT

In the 1950s, a psychologist by the name of Solomon Asch conducted what would become a classic study in group conformity. The active participant was led to believe that he, and the other seven people in the room, were all involved in an experiment on visual judgment. But, the other seven in the room were associates of Asch, and had been given a script to follow. They were directed to answer questions incorrectly, before the active participant had the chance to answer. Asch wanted to see if the individual participant would conform and answer incorrectly, or if they would answer truthfully.

The visual test used was a line test. The participants were simply asked to state which lines they were being shown were the same in length. The majority of the time, the participant answered the same as the group, even when the group answered incorrectly. This is fascinating, because the participant could see with their own eyes that the group was wrong, yet, he went along with the majority.

Interestingly, in some cases one of the members of the group answered correctly. When this happened, the participant was more likely to also answer correctly. They felt they had an ally.

The participants were asked afterwards why they would agree to something their own eyes told them was incorrect. Most said that they knew they were answering wrong, but they went along with the group because they didn't want to be ridiculed, or because they thought they must be wrong if everyone else answered the same way.

The study proved that people conform because they want to fit in with a group, and/or because they believe the group knows more than they do.

* * *

Conformity, giving in to group pressure, is a trait commonly associated with compliance, going along with the majority — even if you don't agree with their beliefs — in order to be accepted.

Steve Forbes is chair, editor-in-chief, and CEO of Forbes Media. Mr. Forbes has been a presidential candidate twice, and has interviewed some of the top CEOs and leaders in the world. Mr. Forbes graciously spoke to me about the role of curiosity in companies and how we need to change our mindset around this in order to foster real innovation.

"People make decisions based on emotion rather than rational thinking," he explained. "What is important is how we respond, and our response is typically based on the lens through which we see the world."

According to Forbes, in order to really break through, "We have to think differently and we need to try and to fail in order to discover new things."

We discussed how trial and error is a form of problem solving that companies need to foster more. This type of exercise typically involves repeated attempts until one is successful. This process can be undermined, however, because of cognitive dissonance, i.e., inconsistent thoughts and actions. One's desire to think differently from the masses may be compromised by the pressure to conform within our environments.

This need to be accepted, Forbes emphasized, causes many people to offer opinions or agree with ideas or decisions that appear popular even if they are not a true reflection of themselves and their personal thoughts or beliefs.

Indeed, many times throughout my career I've seen things done that didn't seem right to me: people promoted for the wrong reasons, people taking credit for someone else's work, decisions being made based on self-interest rather than for the health or goals of the company. But I never said anything — even when I wanted to.

According to Forbes, "People don't want to disagree because they don't want to put their colleagues in jeopardy." Continuing, he said, "People don't want to seem uncollaborative or not spirited. There is a fear among team members in meetings of upsetting the larger group. It is easier to just agree."

Several times in management meetings I vividly recall being reluctant — even fearful — of expressing my thoughts; instead, I went along with the crowd. I was afraid of being talked about as "that employee" who made trouble.

When I was hired at Microsoft, my manager told me that she hired me to drive change. To drive change and to be disruptive requires a willingness to challenge the majority. This will result in tension and disagreement. If you are doing transformational work, it will be next to impossible to not upset anyone. This is the function of the work. People are not okay with change, and so there will be conflict. When intrapreneurs are operating within a company, they are focused on the outcome and are less attentive to what and how others will perceive them. Transformational work is tough. It requires you to fundamentally shift the way current things are being done, and this will cause tension in work environments.

Of course, intrapreneurs do not work alone; they drive change, but they do so while working with others, collaborating with others. They are necessarily part of a team. According to an insightful article by psychologist and author Liane Davey, "In some cultures the language and imagery of teamwork is ridiculously idyllic: rowers in perfect sync, or planes flying in tight formation. As a team, you're 'all in the same boat.' To be a good team player, you must 'row in the same direction.' These idealized versions of teamwork and collaboration are making many teams impotent."*

According to Davey, collaboration without tension, disagreement, or conflict has no purpose. The purpose of collaboration is to improve ideas through competitive back and forth. Others are more likely to see things we aren't — especially if we are invested (and anyone who has an idea is invested in that idea). Of course, any lively back and forth risks exposure and that can lead to tension, resentment, and anger. *Is my idea being attacked, or am I?*

The first thing any leader needs to establish is that ideas are neutral. Discussions and disagreements need to be tailored to that neutrality. How does the idea reach our North Star? We all have to agree about the goal. The means to that end, in other words, is neutral. Will it work? If not, why not? If it might work, how do we improve our chances for success? It is in the nature of successful collaboration to move incrementally from one small step to the next while always having the goal firmly in mind. It is rarely a smooth road. Often it is necessary to take backward steps before we can resume. It is natural to take sides. We are tribal by nature. In a culture where sharing and expressing opinions is encouraged, dissent is necessary and inevitable.

If everyone agrees already, collaboration isn't necessary, right?

Nicholas Thompson, editor-in-chief of *Wired* magazine and contributing editor at CBS and CNN International, has spoken to some of the world's top leaders and thinkers. Speaking to him about the idea of consensus, he told me:

> I don't think that having a lot of consensus is an advantage in companies. If everyone buys in, it is good; people want people to buy into their ideas. If everyone agrees on something, people automatically want to work on it — this is

---

* Liane Davey, "If Your Team Agrees on Everything, Working Together Is Pointless," *Harvard Business Review*, January 31, 2017, hbr.org/2017/01/if-your-team-agrees-on-everything-working-together-is-pointless.

how excitement is created. If smart and capable people work on a project, you will get agreement.

Conformity, on the other hand, has negative connotations. The problem with waiting for a consensus is that you run the risk of missing out on opportunities — things move and change quickly in the marketplace, and especially in the tech industry. So, whether it's a bad decision or a seemingly good decision is irrelevant if it takes too long to come to an agreement on how to proceed. You'll have missed the boat either way.

Achieving consensus not only takes a great deal of time (and for any business time is a precious and costly commodity), but tends to restrain healthy competition and limit efficiency.

Francesca Gino is a behavioural scientist and a professor of business administration at the Harvard Business School. She says, "I hear a lot of people saying as soon as they get into the office they feel the pressure to conform to company culture and norms." Gino wrote an article that appeared in the *Harvard Business Review*, titled "Let Your Workers Rebel."

In the article, she lists three reasons why conformity is so prevalent:

1. We fall prey to social pressure.
2. We become too comfortable with the status quo.
3. We interpret information in a self-serving manner.

She goes on to emphasize the fact that while deviant behaviour is rarely encouraged by leaders, nonconformity actually promotes innovation and improves performance.

Therein lies the problem. Conformity and compliance are innovation assassins. A culture of conformity makes employees afraid to voice ideas, and, frankly, does more harm than good.

Intrapreneurs are not afraid to be disruptive. They challenge the status quo; they believe that conflict is acceptable; and it is within conflict that innovation happens. It is a fundamental belief in the thinking of intrapreneurs that consensus thinking is what inhibits innovation.

## MAJORITY RULE AND CONSENSUS

Is support from the majority important?

Most people think so. In the United States today, for instance, a great debate continues about the "legitimacy" of Donald Trump's election because Hillary Clinton actually won the popular (majority) vote.

Business is no different. What leader wouldn't feel better about moving ahead on a big project if "all hands" voted thumbs up? Well, what about if only three-quarters of the room voted thumbs up? Or half? Truth is, the closer we come to full consensus the more likely it is we will endorse the verdict. Conversely, the farther away from consensus we move, the more likely it will be to doubt or distrust the verdict. It brings up the qualitative distinction between a consensus and a majority.

To achieve a majority, it's only necessary to obtain the support of half plus one; a consensus is much harder to achieve.

Wherever the bar is set, obtaining wide support for a decision sounds like the right way to go, the fair way to go. That may well be, but is it the best way to go for a company that wants to foster a growth mentality and intrapreneurship?

Does striving for majority support or consensus actually work in favour of a company and drive creative thinking, innovation, and big ideas? Does it really move creativity and experimentation forward or does it kill innovation? Does the fact that there is wide support for a decision actually mean that you have reached the right decision?

To drive a culture of innovation from within and to build one of intrapreneurship, allowing for and even seeking out dissent is crucial. Debate sparks innovation. No doubt you have been in meetings where a decision has been agreed upon by the majority, but the support offered has been tepid, lacking enthusiasm. This is usually the result of people agreeing to the decision because of a fear of upsetting teammates and being regarded as the outlier. If dissent is offered, it is too often dismissed as being unconstructive. But dissent is important. It is the outliers who we want to hear from.

One mistake we often make is confusing dissent with disapproval or disagreement.

John Ruffolo is the CEO of OMERS Ventures, one of Canada's leading pension funds, and is widely considered one of the most influential people in the country. His job is to find the next tech unicorn — the thing that's going to disrupt the way we operate as human beings. He is constantly striving to stay fifty steps ahead of the curve. He injects mentorship and capital into these companies to help them realize their vision. The very nature of what he does for a living makes Ruffolo a non-conformist. His purpose is to see the unconventional. To not just spot trends, but to dictate the next big thing in tech. He's backed companies like Hootsuite and Shopify, companies that have contributed to the Canadian economy.

I asked him what he objected to most about conformity.

"It drives me nuts when people conform. When I don't hear the debate, I know there is fear."

The problem, he insisted, begins and ends with leadership. "Leaders with massive insecurity … think they have all the answers, and don't want dissent."

If fear of dissent is such a systemic problem in companies, I wondered, what is the solution?

"If I'm with my team, and we're sitting around the table, I look around and ensure that the most senior person gives their perspective last. Why? Because I don't want people feeling afraid to express their thoughts. I ask people directly, 'Do you agree with everything that has been said?' If they say yes, I say: 'How can that be?' I force the debate. I want people to disagree. The debate is the most important thing. When there is debate, this is where the magic happens."

## CONFLICT

You don't want to create a culture of nonconformity — you want to create a culture where there is a freedom of ideas and where people can disagree. If you avoid disagreement, there is a risk that weak ideas or assumptions will go unnoticed.

As a result of my research and my interviews with big thinkers, including Ruffolo, I have come to the conclusion that if you want to empower your teams, you must do the following:

1. **Force debate.** In most companies, there is an unhealthy reluctance to allow internal debate and dissent. Ruffolo says, "I love the fight. I think

more highly of people when they push back on me and force me to articulate my perspective." Reward the whole team for the debate; encourage more disagreement. If you are the leader in a room of people and everyone agrees, ask, '*Why* do you agree? What is your perspective?' Give people the opportunity to really speak their minds. Different points of view come out and perspectives become stronger and better developed. When you only hear what people think you want to hear, you miss out on a lot of important information. You've blocked yourself from the truth, and the truth is what any business really needs to thrive.

2. **Eliminate repercussions.** Leaders need to create safe environments where people can disagree — nobody should be reprimanded for disagreeing. Without the fear of repercussions, people will be more likely to speak their minds. Take a look at the power dynamics among the team members that could create fear. When leaders start to disagree with each other it may equalize the room. When leaders start to agree with the minority, it may equalize the room. Leaders need to create this environment. You need to truly demonstrate that you want dissent.

3. **Show vulnerability.** Leaders don't need to be superheroes. Leaders are human, and they need to be seen by everyone in the company as flawed. What people tend to reward the most from their leaders is fairness and consistency. You don't need to have all the answers; you do need to be fair and consistent. Find the North Star and stick to it. Be as truthful and transparent as possible. If you can, let your guard down. We all make mistakes. It's okay for leaders to ask for help. What isn't okay is pretending to have an expertise you don't possess. When leaders are honest and admit to making mistakes it opens doors to experimentation. "Well, that didn't work. I goofed. Does anybody have a better idea?" Elicit feedback and learn how to listen effectively. At the end of the day, we're all in this together, right?

Innovation thrives where rules are not imposed, where different ways of thinking and doing things are encouraged. It is in the depths of conflict that you'll find new ideas. Expressing varying opinions actually creates more ideas. As *Forbes*'s Rajamannar told me, "If people disagree, we duke it out, we have full transparency and call out passive aggressive behaviour."

If we equip our teams to focus on ideas rather than on people, this will yield the right output. Rather than creating an atmosphere where employees are caught up creating allies, create an atmosphere where great ideas can be cultivated. This is the real shift that needs to happen. Focus on what the goals are.

Nicholas Thompson shared some truly insightful words with me when we spoke. He said that his specialty is trying to figure out a way to produce creative stories and high-quality journalism. That is his North Star, his guiding principle. He is focused on outcomes. "I look at things from a values perspective and try to align my editorial goals to my business goals. In the end, we want to do our best work." Encouraging employees to focus on goals motivates people to offer their own ideas, to offer dissent, to think about creative ways on how to solve problems — without getting caught up by fear or other distracting influences.

When your company and the people who work for you are all working together, focused on outcomes, that's when the best work is done. Rather than worrying about people and politics, worry about the work. Do the work! It's about what the people are working together to achieve. Conflict is good, challenging ideas is good, debating is good. The goal is to encourage risk, encourage ideas, and at the same time encourage all to question those ideas in order to make better decisions. Focus on outputs.

# CHAPTER FOUR

## Curiosity ... Did It Really Kill the Cat?

Unfortunately the highly curious student is a small percentage of the kids.

— Bill Gates

CHARAN RANGANATH IS a psychologist and researcher interested in why we're able to retain some things and forget others. According to his research, our brain's chemistry changes when we're curious.* When our curiosity is piqued, we experience a dopamine release, and we get an actual high.

When we're curious, he said, there's increased activity in our hippocampus — the part of our brain that helps us create memories. Furthermore, when we're intrigued, we become better at learning, even bits of information we don't really find interesting.

I am curious by nature. Frankly, I think most people are. Watch almost any infant anywhere and what do you see? Huge eyes staring wonderingly at the world. *Who is that? What is that? Where did that come from? Where is it going?*

We don't question the natural curiosity of a child. We encourage it — even when, as a parent, we are weary to the point of tears hearing that question for the millionth time: *How come?*

---

* Mark D'Esposito and Bradley R. Postle, "The Cognitive Neuroscience of Working Memory," *Annual Review of Psychology*, no. 66 (January 2015): 115–42, ncbi.nlm.nih.gov/pmc/articles/PMC4374359/.

When I brought my natural curiosity to my professional career, I quickly learned that the practice of asking questions was problematic. Why? Because if you ask questions, people believe that you doubt the worth of the explanations and ideas presented to you. They feel threatened that their authority is being challenged. People who are curious are labelled as "difficult" or "high maintenance." I've been there multiple times. During a performance review in a former job, a manager informed me that my peers thought I was high maintenance.

I was stunned. And hurt. "Why? What does that mean?" I asked him for examples.

Well, he said, I was always asking questions and challenging the way things were done. Instead of accepting the criticism as a compliment, I decided to conform. I stopped asking questions. I resisted querying colleagues about procedures and practices. I domesticated my instincts and muted my curiosity mode. I stopped sharing insights or ideas and never offered any more opinions about anything. It was a horrible period. Eventually I left the company.

It took me a long time to realize that I wasn't the problem; it was the company that was at fault. When they asked me for my opinions or insights, what they really wanted was my approval.

## BUT ... CURIOSITY KILLED THE CAT

No great innovation happened without someone asking a simple question: Why not? But we all have had our own experiences like the cat of the infamous proverb. It happened to me; it still does. Asking too many questions — being too curious — leads to trouble. Better to keep your mouth shut and your head down. Don't make waves.

No!

Where would we be if humans were not naturally curious? To be curious means to question things. To be skeptical. To always be asking why. Without curiosity, we would have no penicillin, no space travel, no red wine.

Without curiosity, how would we learn? How would we have any innovation at all?

This is why it's so puzzling to me that in the corporate world curiosity is seen as a negative trait. If you've ever been in a meeting room, you know this is true. In art, science, and preschool, curiosity is seen as a positive thing. But in the corporate world, it is perceived as deviance, as an act of rebellion. For businesses to thrive in our current corporate climate, this must change.

I can't help but be curious, so I keep drilling down to the issue and asking more questions until I truly understand the issue at hand — until I have all of the information I need to make a solid decision.

The ideal intrapreneur always questions the why. Intrapreneurs are always asking why things are as they are, how things can be improved, and what there is to be discovered. They are cultivators of ideas. What I mean by this is that because of their curious selves, they take seeds of ideas and they germinate them into sustainable creative plans. They do all the research, analysis, deep thinking behind them, and cultivate them into plans that are executable within companies.

## THE FORCE THAT DRIVES INNOVATION

After dropping out of college to save his parents the tuition costs, Steve Jobs decided to enroll himself in a class on typography. Sounds like an odd thing for a college dropout to do, but Jobs was curious about calligraphy. He wanted to learn more about what makes some typefaces so great, and others so boring. Was it the spacing? The size? The boldness? Serif? Sans-serif? So he started studying the topic of typography.

Ten years later, Jobs designed the first Mac computer, and guess what? It came with a variety of fonts — something the average computer user was not used to. This became a key differentiator for Apple, and it literally changed the way we write.

Leonardo da Vinci, best known as a painter of masterpieces, had an insatiable curiosity that extended far beyond the conventional world of art. He conducted autopsies, created sculptures, invented flying machines — he even improved on the design of the clock by using springs rather than weights. He was a man deeply interested in science, technology, and art. Da Vinci didn't identify as a scientist, an inventor, or an artist. He lived with the belief that everything is connected, so therefore, all subjects are related.

Individuals who follow their curiosities are naturally able to solve problems by making connections between the issue at hand and things they've learned along the way.

Einstein said, "I have no special talent. I am only passionately curious."

When you encourage your people to be curious, you will have more creative teams. When we are curious, our brains are constantly trying to make connections.

If you're not encouraging a climate of inquisitiveness, you might be losing your da Vincis and Einsteins — your best talent. Your most curious employees are likely being viewed as troublemakers. They're probably not being taken seriously or given promotions. Your curious employees are most likely miserable and looking for new opportunities.

Whenever curiosity is welcomed in a society or a company, open-mindedness tends to follow. Any company that welcomes curiosity will be a successful company. After all, curiosity is the path we follow to navigate the unknown ... it's the path that leads to innovation.

When I talked to Steve Forbes, he mentioned that we need something called positive anxiety to remain curious. We are used to thinking about anxiety in a negative sense. That familiar feeling of being tense and uncomfortable, where we get those butterflies in our stomach when we start a new job, enroll in a new course, or have to deliver a pitch or presentation. Healthy anxiety motivates us to do our best work. It forces us to prepare, to dig deeper, and it keeps us on our toes. This type of anxious feeling is natural and pushes us to do our best. It makes us stay ahead of the curve.

This also forces us to always be thinking. When we are thinking, our radar is on, we see things happening, we are observant of changes, and this all keeps us grounded and in tune with our environments.

Bill Gates and Warren Buffet are two of the wealthiest and best-known entrepreneurs in the world. And both men cite curiosity as their most important quality. Gates encourages people to continue learning throughout their lives. He's been quoted as saying, "A lot of people lose their curiosity as they get older, which is a shame." Buffet reads at least five hundred pages of a book each and every day. "That's how knowledge works. It builds up, like compound interest. All of you can do it, but I guarantee not many of you will do it."

People are afraid of not looking smart when they ask too many questions, but Gates says, "Smartness is not single-dimensional and not quite as important as I thought it was."

How can you foster a culture of curiosity in your teams?

1.  **Be observant.** Ethnography is the study and recording of human culture and behaviour. I urge you to become an ethnographer. There is great power in observation — observing the world around you can lead to creative breakthroughs. If you want true data points, you must be observant. Watch people. Study how they eat, how they work, how they interact, how they communicate. Go into a coffee shop and see how people are using technology, how they are working. Go into a retail environment and see how people are using their smartphones when making purchases. Go into a restaurant and see how people are interacting. Be curious. The more curious you are, the more you notice. Become a walking ethnographer and take the information you're learning and apply it in meaningful ways in your business.

2.  **Engage with people and stay in the moment.** When is the last time you zoned out during a conversation? How often do you end up distracted by your phone during a meeting? I find this is happening more and more often because we are so unfocused. If you make an effort to stay engaged with people, you will soon realize that we have a lot to learn from each other by simply listening. In my last place of work, we had a "no cellphones in meetings" rule. When you put away the phones you eliminate distractions and raise engagement. With more engagement, you have more interest and questions flow organically. Be in the practice of active listening. Be curious about the experiences and thoughts of others. This will bring new insights and new creativity.

3.  **Question everything.** There are usually two kinds of people in a meeting: those who believe there's no such thing as a dumb or bad question, and those who play it safe and are scared to talk. The greatest creative minds — think of da Vinci, Einstein, and Jobs — question everything. Creative entrepreneurs and leaders foster environments that encourage creativity and exploration of conflicting viewpoints.

4.  **Read.** I am constantly reading. Whether perusing articles or scanning books, I pursue ideas — ideas that open my mind and help me see things from a different perspective. I minimize reading the news because it depresses me, but I read articles — academic, business, culture. I carve out one hour a day in the morning to read.

Raja Rajamannar summed up the role that curiosity plays in driving innovation beautifully when he said, "We are never in a state of perfection; we need to find new and better ways of doings things."

The world is ever-changing. We are in a state of disruption and companies are being displaced. So, this pursuit of constantly finding new and better ways makes total sense. "Try something new," Rajamannar says, "it will not always be perfect, but part of this process is failing and learning."

The quest for perfection can be paralyzing. It won't happen. Good is better than perfect, right? I will discuss this idea in more detail in a later chapter, but for now I would like to stress that it's crucial for businesses to get past the idea of perfection. It doesn't exist, and businesses need to also approach innovation from a point of view of fluidity, to understand and embrace the fact that the world is ever-changing. Nothing is constant. Nothing is perfect. It will always need to evolve.

Steve Forbes said that we need to rise and fall in order to discover. Our human nature makes us want to stay in our comfort zone, but we must rise to achieve and discover. We are wired in such a way to stay with what is familiar, but we all know that it is within unfamiliar territory where learning happens most.

Rajamannar reinforces this point by saying, "Anything new makes you uncomfortable, but the danger is to be complacent."

Many pundits have cited complacency as the main reason for some failed businesses. When complacency takes root in a company's culture, it is often fatal.

We have seen this over and over again with the rise and fall of many great companies: Sears, Danier, Blockbuster Video, BlackBerry. All failed because they didn't anticipate and embrace change. They became complacent.

It is always good to have nervous energy — to be on your toes, to maybe have some healthy anxiety when it comes to the business; complacency silently chips away at companies. Rajamannar states, "We should never be married to an idea or thought. You need to let it go when things are not working."

As much as we have to focus on what we are doing, we need to also make informed decisions on what we will stop doing. Companies often become focused on what they should do, but they should also focus on what they shouldn't do.

"Now you see companies going back to their core competencies," Forbes said in an interview. He mentioned Microsoft as a perfect example.

Microsoft was the most valuable company in the world, but then it lost focus in the marketplace when it tried to be everything to everyone. When Microsoft jumped the phone market, for instance, the company foundered. It bought Nokia, and things went downhill. Its efforts to go into devices failed. Luckily, management recognized the problem and reversed course. It went back to the basics and refocused its efforts and reinforced its position in the software market. It reclaimed relevance by being among the first to exploit cloud technology. It got back to and strengthened its commitment to its core competencies (software and smart office products).

Admitting defeat took guts. But it was the right move. The company had lost track of its North Star. Charlie Munger, a partner with Warren Buffett for many years and a stunningly successful investor in his own right, talks about the need to understand a "core competency." Basically, he knows what his is and never strays outside it. Innovation isn't only about doing something new. It more often can be all about doing something you are already doing, but doing it better.

The fact that Microsoft abandoned new areas of its business and returned to its core competencies may not seem to be an example of creative thinking, of intrapreneurship. But it is. Microsoft had evolved into a large, inefficient, and increasingly less profitable company. It took creative thinking to look at the situation, determine what was working and what wasn't, and envision a new, leaner company, one that focused on its strengths and built from those. Microsoft changed itself in order to better succeed in a changing marketplace. You must be willing to do the same. Remember what Rajamannar said, "Don't be married to an idea. If it isn't working, let it go."

Imagining something new, even a new version of old, requires looking beyond the obvious, beyond the now. It requires curiosity, an interest in what is and what could be. Curiosity is the heart of all of this — it is the soul of what drives these behaviours. If you are curious, that means that you are "never settling for the status quo."

But what if you do settle? "If this is the case," said Raja Rajamannar, "then you are at risk of obsolescence, which will require you to be future proof."

# CHAPTER FIVE

## First Principles Thinking

We get through life by reasoning by analogy, which essentially means copying what other people do with slight variations. With first principles you boil things down to the most fundamental truths ... and then reason up from there.

— Elon Musk

A SKEPTIC IS SOMEONE who questions whether or not it is possible to know something with absolute certainty. Seventeenth-century French scientist and philosopher René Descartes was such a skeptic that there was a form of skepticism named after him: Cartesian skepticism.

When Descartes came to the realization that many things he once believed wholeheartedly to be true could not be proven to be so beyond doubt, he was greatly distraught. He wondered, what do I know and how do I *really know* that I know it? All knowledge was a flimsy house of cards that rested on foundations of air!

He decided the only way to be sure he was not committed to false beliefs was to disbelieve absolutely everything until he could prove it to be true.

Descartes used the analogy of a basket of apples. If there was even one rotten apple in the basket, it could spoil all the apples. Assumptions were like the bad apple.

\* \* \*

Intrapreneurs go to the heart of a problem when trying to determine truths. They never make assumptions, knowing that assumptions are simply that, and that facts and data are always what will prove to be the gateway to the most accurate decisions and outcomes.

When I worked at TELUS, I was involved in a very special project called "Upopolis" — a private social network developed for Canadian children in hospitals to help normalize their lives. Upopolis would facilitate communication between children and their teachers, their friends, and their family members at home. A wonderful initiative, but when the project hit my desk, it was in only one hospital in Canada. The project had been passed around from person to person, and nobody wanted to work on it. Upopolis was deemed problematic, and it had lain dormant for months.

I was told the whole platform needed to be "redone." It was built on poor technology, it was "unusable," and hospitals had "lost interest."

I took the project over and started to peel back the layers. I went back to the very beginning, did some research, started asking questions. I found out who the engineers on the project were, and I spoke to them about what was wrong with the technology. There were fifty outstanding software issues it turned out, so I began making phone calls and speaking with people. I built up a small, dedicated team. We went through every single problem one by one. Some were problems that had already been solved, and some were legitimate problems that we assigned engineers to fix.

The main issue with Upopolis was that the project had lost focus. Many things that were deemed to be wrong with it were not, in fact, problems. People had just come to believe that they were. They had made assumptions.

Within a couple of months, we had solved all fifty issues. We then had a solid platform we could continue to deploy throughout hospitals in Canada.

We approached it from a very simple mindset. We went back to the beginning. What do you like about Upopolis? What could be better? What more could we do so that kids will use it? From there, we built a project plan and decided how we were going to tackle it.

We had to stabilize the platform, create some interest, develop a deployment plan, and come up with an enhancement plan. We broke the plan into tasks with assigned responsibilities and dates so that we knew who was accountable for what. Slowly but surely, the plan was executed.

Our next task was to create interest. We reached out to hospitals. We made phone calls, set up meetings, and introduced administration to our new platform. Within a year and a half we were deployed in eighty percent of children's hospitals in Canada, including SickKids — one of the largest children's hospitals in North America. The project was a success; in fact, we were awarded the ITAC Corporate Heroes Award. Upopolis, once a program that was assumed to be irrelevant, had become a core pillar of TELUS's corporate social responsibility initiatives.

People made a number of assumptions about Upopolis that were simply not true.

Asking the right questions and going back to fundamental issues allowed us to set this project on the right path. I believe that this method, when practised with diligence, can set companies on the right trajectory to make better-informed decisions.

\* \* \*

A fundamental flaw in many companies is that when making important decisions we *assume* we are dealing with facts. Often, we're not. We're making assumptions. Once an assumption enters the common currency of a company's culture it is very difficult to root out as counterfeit. It looks and feels just like a fact.

In a world of high assumption-to-knowledge ratios, it is all too common and too easy to fall down giant rabbit holes into a world of fantasy. Hard work is needed to replace fantasy with reality. When that happens, truths are revealed.

Here are some common assumptions I've heard over the years:

- There is not a market for it.
- It is too complicated.
- It will never be approved.

- That will be too time-consuming.
- That will be too expensive to create.
- You cannot scale it.
- That idea has already been done.

An assumption-based culture discourages proactive and creative approaches to performance. Assumptions are like lies. Once they have been uttered it's hard to take them back. Even worse, assumptions gather momentum; this is especially true when they justify the negative — like poor performance or lacklustre sales. It probably comes as no surprise that the companies that defend rule-based policies and procedures the most aggressively are the ones that are most dependent on assumptions. When there is much to lose, there is much to defend.

## BELIEFS AND ASSUMPTIONS

Our assumptions are the result of ideas and beliefs we've inherited over our lifetime. Our assumptions become so ingrained in us that we don't question them. True or not, we accept and believe these things to be true.

As humans we naturally and regularly use our beliefs and assumptions to navigate our world. We must do so to make sense of where we are, what we're about, and what is happening around us. We make assumptions when we don't fully understand situations. We naturally tend to fill in bits of missing information by making up our own story ... to make sense of things.

The problem is that most of the time, our assumptions — the stories we tell ourselves — are simply inaccurate.

I can't help but wonder how many great innovations were stopped in their tracks due to assumptions.

## FIRST PRINCIPLES THINKING

As we defined it earlier, a first principle is a brute fact that cannot be reduced any further. Think of it as a brick as opposed to a wall composed of bricks. First principles thinking involves analyzing a complicated problem and breaking it down to its basic issues. You can then work to solve these basic issues, which will in turn solve your initial problem. This is just as

Descartes described with his apple basket analogy. This strategy exposes fundamental truths and encourages original solutions.

When Elon Musk was told that electric cars were too expensive for the average person to buy, he went Cartesian, and instead of accepting the knowledge of the crowd, applied first principles thinking. He explained his process in an interview with Digg founder and GV, formerly Google Ventures, partner Kevin Rose: "Somebody could — and people do — say battery packs are really expensive and that's just the way they always will be because that's the way they have been in the past."

Can you see the flaw in that reasoning? How will we ever create things that never existed before if we base our innovations on old assumptions or preconceived ideas?

In that interview, Musk said, "If you applied that reasoning to anything new then you would never be able to get to that new thing. You can't say, 'Oh, nobody wants a car because horses are great and we're used to them, and there's grass all over the place, so people will never buy cars.' And people did say that. For batteries, they would say, 'Oh, historically, it has cost $600 per kilowatt hour, and so it's not going to get much better than that in the future.'"

Musk explained that when he applied first principles thinking to this issue he started to strip down the problems. He asked, "What are the batteries made of? What is the value of the components?" By doing that he broke things down and discovered that if he bought the different components separately, batteries would cost only $80 per kilowatt hour.

When you break a complex problem down to its basic components, examine each and every one individually to see if earlier conclusions about them are, in fact, true, rather than based on assumption, you're applying first principles thinking. And first principles thinking will always help you find more efficient and creative ways of doing things.

## CLEARBANC

Clearbanc is a FinTech (financial technology) company co-founded by Andrew D'Souza, Michele Romanow, and Charlie Feng. Broadly speaking, FinTech is an emerging industry where technology is applied in the financial services industry. This technology is used to help companies manage the financial aspects of their business, including new software, applications, processes, and business models. FinTech, in essence, is modernizing traditional financial services methods. Clearbanc provides funding to entrepreneurs in the sharing economy (Uber, Airbnb). Funds are provided in the form of an advance, not a loan. Unlike big banks, which make lending decisions based on assumptions, Clearbanc uses a special revenue forecasting engine that analyzes real data, like the business's history, its user reviews, and actual earnings. There's no credit check involved. Clearbanc's model involves using first principles thinking, peeling back the layers and determining whether an entrepreneur is a solid investment or not.

I had the opportunity to sit down with one of Clearbanc's co-founders, Michele Romanow, who is also a Canadian venture capitalist, tech entrepreneur, and CBC Dragon. Romanow is on the list of 100 Most Powerful Women in Canada, recognized by the Women Executives Network, and was named as one of the *Forbes* Top 20 Most Disruptive "Millennials on a Mission."

"If someone asks you if you went to the gym this morning," she said, when we sat down for an interview, "you may say, 'No, I slept in, but I really wanted to work out,' but that's not true. You didn't really want to go, you wanted to sleep in, otherwise you would have worked out."

Romanow explained that we answer that way because we think we should want to exercise. This is the same reason that we answer survey questions the way we think the survey wants us to answer. We feel like we're being watched, so we think we need to answer the way the surveyor wants us to respond. She believes we only behave authentically when we're not being watched.

For Romanow, one of the main sources of innovation blockage in large companies is the lack of freedom given to people to dig to the roots of problems. Employees are in constant firefighting mode — obsessed with short-term targets and deliverables. As a result, people don't know how to be innovative. They make assumptions rather than ask questions, because doing so makes them feel like they are being efficient and productive. Nobody is peeling back the layers to get to the truth of an issue. This process is time-consuming. But what if the truth is down one more layer?

\* \* \*

Humans are terrible predictors of success, and this is why assumptions are not effective in business. Who would have believed people would rent out space in their primary homes to strangers? People may rent their secondary residences, but there was an assumption that nobody would rent their primary homes. But that was an assumption. Look at Airbnb.

You need to stop making assumptions and start applying first principles thinking instead. Here's how you can start to do this in your company.

1. **Ask the why.** Romanow says that we must always ask why. Why this? Why is it done this way? Grind your way through solving problems. Ask your why four times in a row. You must go back and keep asking until you're at the core of the problem and the nut is cracked. "We make assumptions because it is easy and not enough people are asking questions. It feels like we are being efficient when we make assumptions, but it often makes us revisit work.

2. **Apply the process of iteration.** You must allow your employees to iterate, to drill down, and to work through problems. You can't base important decisions on assumptions — assumptions that something is too expensive or too difficult or too time-consuming. Remove all of the doubts and base your decisions on facts.

3. **Focus more on execution.** Apply five to ten percent of your thinking to strategy and the rest toward execution. We need to allow our teams to ask big questions, test, learn, and execute. When we spend too much time thinking *against* or *around* ideas instead of *into* ideas — finding out where they lead — we get stuck. We need to realize that to succeed it is crucial to only spend a small percentage of the time allotted to solving a problem on strategy; the rest of the time should be spent getting things done. This is where the facts will start to reveal truths on how to make work move.

First principles thinking will revolutionize the way you solve problems and the way you do business. If you stop basing your decisions on assumptions, and instead boil ideas down to facts, imagine the innovation that will be possible. Remember, it is impossible to create something that has never existed before if we rely on assumptions and existing ideas.

Now that we've explored the concepts of rules, consensus, curiosity, and assumptions, it is time for us to move on to the next part of *The Greenhouse Approach,* where I will take you through the seven guiding principles I believe will future-proof your company.

# PART TWO

# THE MODEL

# CHAPTER SIX

## The Seven Guiding Principles

It is not the strongest of the species that survives, nor the most intelligent that survives. It is the one that is most adaptable to change.

— Charles Darwin

IN THE 1990s, a herd of Cape buffalo and a subspecies of lions became stranded on a small island that had become detached from mainland Africa.* The lions had no other food source, and Cape buffalo, with their large stature, incredible strength, and deadly hooves and horns, are not easy prey. The lions should not have survived, but they did because the lions adapted.

The lions were forced to develop sophisticated hunting techniques so they could catch and eat the only food source they had available to them. They began to develop ways of coordinating their hunting efforts to increase their odds of surviving. They learned the daily habits of the buffalo, and so became able to predict when the herd would need to stop moving to get water.

The lions separated into three groups. One pride of lions would stalk the herd of buffalo, corralling them and taking down weak or injured members. Another pride became strong swimmers and learned to hunt from

* Zoe Brennan, "The Superlions Marooned on an Island," *Daily Mail*, June 24, 2006, http://www.dailymail.co.uk/news/article-392292/The-superlions-marooned-island.html.

deep waters, which lions normally don't do. When a buffalo went to the water's edge for a drink, a lion would be waiting underwater, ready to take a deadly swipe with a paw. Another pride of aggressive lions would simply tackle a buffalo in a fight to the death.

This physical activity and steady diet of buffalo meat led to these lions developing huge muscles. The cats adapted to become larger and stronger, becoming what some have called "superlions."

In order to increase their chances of survival, the buffalo also adapted. They began travelling in large mega-herds of 1,200 or more, and when one of the herd was sick, weak, and had to rest, the entire group would cluster, horns facing outwards, to protect themselves from the lions.

Interestingly, the lions continued to prey on the weak and vulnerable buffalo, effectively purging the herd of the least fit. Overall, it was a win for both sides. Not good news if you happen to be a weak or sick buffalo, of course, but nature is both imaginatively resourceful and coldly unsentimental.

$$* * *$$

In nature, animals who cannot adapt, die. And it's no different in business. Companies need to adapt themselves to changes in the marketplace, in technology, and to increasing competition.

Adapt or die? Is it really that serious? Well, you wouldn't be reading this book if you didn't already know the answer.

Companies today must be able to adapt to times of change. To pivot, learn to do new things, and remain relevant in order to survive. It is the same truth in nature and in business. It is the intrapreneurs within your companies that will enable your companies to become more adaptable. These people have the talents, traits, and conviction to help you sustain and anticipate changes in the market.

The business world is a jungle, an environment in which only those who can adapt fast enough can survive.

## ADAPTATION THEORY FOR BUSINESS

Individuals and companies must be able to adapt in order to succeed in a rapidly changing environment. But, having an ability to adapt is not enough. Businesses and companies must be able to see what is ahead, look for trends, and anticipate what is coming next based on the changing behaviour of consumers and the marketplace. In a best-case scenario, they should be able to drive change themselves, taking the lead and forcing others to adapt to the new reality that they have created.

To anticipate change so that you are proactive rather than reactive, you need to do three things.

1. **Be aware of the current situation within your company.** What is the current state of the business? What is the purpose of the company? What is the status of your customers? Are they satisfied? Are their needs being met, or are they changing? The answers to these questions can easily change as demographics change and new markets and audiences form. Are there new markets that your business could capture? The world has changed; new markets have emerged, including millennials, single parents, DINKs (double income, no kids), LGBTQ2 individuals, as well as all sorts of new socio-economic classes. Different ethnic groups now form important parts of the cultural mosaic. Do they apply to you? Has your customer based changed? Have their needs evolved? Do they buy differently? Do they interact and communicate differently? What is going on with new entrants to the market? How are they competing and what are they offering your customer base that you are not? Asking these questions is crucial, and it is your intrapreneurs, the thinkers, the researchers in your company, who will take the lead on this.

   All of these variables could impact your current infrastructure and how you support and service your customers. You must understand and embrace change, equipping your companies with the tools, skills, and knowledge needed to adapt.

2. **Look at your products and services.** Have you become complacent? Are your services still resonating with your customers? Have their needs and desires changed? Are there new entrants to the market that have better products? Should you be concerned?

   We are often selective about what we see and hear, reluctant to expose ourselves to what may not be working, in fear of change. Knowing that we have to change and having the awareness of all of the work that will come along with that is daunting. Inertia obviously is dangerous, so you must shift your mindset to embrace change. To succeed, you need to anticipate the new and stay ahead of the curve, constantly researching, observing, and forecasting what is coming next ... if not creating it.

You must cultivate an outside-in view, not just taking in information but also using it in a meaningful way. This will enable companies to have a clear competitive advantage over those who suffer from insularity.

3. **Re-imagine change.** Change is inevitable. Instead of fighting change, embrace it and ride the wave. You need to realize that the wave is coming and learn how to ride it rather than drown in it.

   This means you must know and understand which parts of your company will be impacted by those waves. Are these changes going to impact your workforce? Will they impact parts of your operations and how you support your customers? Will change impact how work gets done? If you can identify which elements of your business will be impacted by change, it will be easier for you to get your head around it all. If you think of change as a new mode of operation, it will make it easier to pivot and switch directions, and to do it with grace and confidence, staying focused on the desired outcomes.

It is important to understand that in this fast-changing environment and marketplace, skills and knowledge become old very quickly. It is therefore essential to be a constant learner. Bill Gates has said that he will always be a life learner. Why? Because he believes that learning is the single best investment of time that we can make.

Benjamin Franklin said, "An investment in knowledge pays the best interest." The fact of the matter is that we are in a knowledge economy. People who have intellect, if leveraged properly, can turn that knowledge into financial capital.

Learning opens your mind to adaptability. You must develop a learning mindset. Many companies are shifting their cultures in this way, to encourage this in their employees, and to set themselves up for adaptability. Remember the quote from Warren Buffett about reading? He said reading was like compounding interest. But he also predicted that while anyone could read, most wouldn't. Here's one of the world's savviest and most successful investors predicting that most aspiring business people won't do what they need to do to be successful: *remain curious and keep learning.*

Satya Nadella, CEO of Microsoft, has been working to transform the culture of the company. He famously said that we must shift from "a know-it-all to be a learn-it-all." What this means essentially is that everyone should be a student, in constant learning mode. If you proclaim that you know it all already, you are limiting your capability to learn more. You need to be constantly accessing new information and ideas. We are in an information age, access to information is a new form of value currency.

## CULTURE, LEARNING, AND CAPITAL

Futurist Peter Diamandis has written about something he calls rapid demonetization.*

With the rise of technology, automation, and mass production, many things that were once expensive to produce are now cheap, thanks to technological advances. While goods and services may decrease in monetary value, knowledge is becoming more and more valuable. This will continue to happen, with new technology being introduced to the world, such as artificial intelligence and quantum computing.

What will be left for humans, if everything is going to be automated and outsourced to AI (artificial intelligence)? If machines can think for us, what will be the value that humans bring to the world? What makes us human — what makes us different — is our capacity for creativity, compassion, intuition, and heart. We can't teach a robot how to be creative, or how to solve problems creatively. Intellectual capital — knowledge — is what will become the most valuable commodity in the world of business, and everything else will be taken over by technology.

A debate is raging about which skills artificial intelligence will replace and how technology will eliminate millions of jobs worldwide in the years

* Vanessa Bates Ramirez, "The 6 Ds of Tech Disruption: A Guide to the Digital Economy," (Singularity University: 2016), singularityhub.com/2016/11/22/the-6-ds-of-tech-disruption-a-guide-to-the-digital-economy/#sm.0000a8htqk9fvelfznh2mx6isdttr.

ahead. We know that robots and AI already are taking over jobs like data collection and processing, and are moving into the types of tasks geared toward doing a mass amount of computation and synthesization.

Skills that technology will not be able to replace are creative thinking, judgment, and problem solving. With a creative mind and imagination, you can invent something totally new. You can blend your own personal experiences, emotions, and knowledge to devise something — a product, a service, an idea — that has never existed before. Robots don't have personal experiences or emotions; these are what set us apart, what define us as human beings. Creating associations of ideas, concepts, and information leads to creativity.

Of course, imagination and creativity are not the only elements necessary to create and run a successful program or business. Practical matters also need to be considered. To find the right balance between these elements requires judgment. To exercise good judgment is to make a sound decision or to draw sensible conclusions. Some may argue that robots are able to do this; I would argue, however, that is untrue. Part of what makes humans good decision-makers is our ability to see the facts while at the same time leveraging our intuition, our imagination. Some people refer to it as a feeling or your gut. In the interviews that I conducted in my research, one CEO spoke about the role of intuition in leading. He told me that at times, even if the data showed one thing, his intuition told him to do the polar opposite and, well, his gut was right. This kind of quality or trait is innate to humans.

\* \* \*

I have developed a problem-solving methodology that incorporates both creativity and practical concerns. I've spent twenty years in the corporate world, and every project or initiative I've worked on has been problem-led. I believe that regardless of what industry or discipline that we are in, we are all in the business of solving problems.

Through my research, reading, observations, and interviews, consistent themes and ideas have emerged. These are the guiding principles that inform my model for problem solving, a model that harnesses judgment and creativity, the twin elements of intrapreneurship, to foster change and, ultimately, success. These guiding principles will give you the context and rationale for my model.

The seven guiding principles are:

1.  Relevance
2.  Creativity
3.  Speed
4.  Clarity
5.  Accountability
6.  Experimentation
7.  Execution

In the next chapter, we will explore the seven guiding principles in deeper detail. Each principle represents the rationale for why we need intrapreneurs.

# CHAPTER SEVEN

## Relevance

SONY ONCE OWNED the music industry. It had its own music label. It made its own music players. In the 1980s and 90s, it seemed like every teenager either had or coveted a Sony Walkman (later, a Sony Discman). Sony had what seemed like a huge advantage heading into the digital music age, but when cassettes and CDs fell out of favour, when devices such as iPhones and services such as online streaming took over the market, Sony completely missed the boat.

Why did it fail to remain relevant? Was it too big to move quickly? Did it lose its connection to its customers?

In a desperate Hail Mary to retain dwindling market share, Sony launched a music subscription service as a challenge to upstart rival iTunes. It flopped. Customers greeted Sony's offering with a thunderous yawn. What happened? Sony not only occupied the top of the mountain — it *was* the mountain.

The company lost its connection; it suddenly had turned deaf to the market's desires. The music giant waited so long to embrace change that by the time it recovered its mojo it was too late. Sony was obsolete, like eight-track, cassettes, and Blu-ray. And to anyone watching, the scariest thing was how fast it all happened. Sure, Sony is still a very successful company, with interests in many areas, but it no longer has any meaningful presence in the music player market. One thing you can say about companies like Apple: they aren't afraid of innovation.

\* \* \*

Once upon a time, all it took for a business to thrive was a great product or service, good marketing, and cool branding. Not anymore. Consumers are becoming more fickle. We have so much in the way of choice; there are temptations around every corner. There are so many networks for consumers to tap into if they are looking for something new, and the rate at which we make decisions is alarmingly fast.

Since the dawn of the digital revolution and the creation of the internet, the world has changed profoundly. The internet has changed how we shop, how we plan our meals, how we communicate, how we learn, and how we live. The internet has also led to globalization, bringing a worldwide marketplace to consumers' fingertips. As a result, businesses are struggling to remain relevant.

The digital revolution is further elevating the difficulty for businesses to remain relevant. In this brave new world, with augmented reality, self-driving cars, robotics, artificial intelligence, and a number of other types of exciting technological breakthroughs, how will your business stay in the hearts and minds of consumers? By embracing technology to better understand the market, customers, and data.

Companies using technology the right way will win.

When did you last flip through the Yellow Pages to look up a phone number? I certainly haven't done so in years. Like anyone else with a mobile phone, I tend to search numbers that I need from my device. This one-hundred-year-old company desperately needed to re-establish its relevance to its market in a digital economy. People once relied on the iconic brand of print directories, but former customers were now seeking information online. And so the company switched gears, ditching the published directories it once produced and, instead, offering the information it provided via YP.ca — an online platform. YP was Yellow Pages' effort to remain relevant, to re-imagine their traditional way of doing business, to cater to new markets. They recognized the changing needs of their customers, and took steps to become relevant again.

YP is not simply an online version of the old publication. Today, when a new advertiser signs up with YP, it is offered a wide range of support services for its marketing needs, well beyond the Yellow Pages site. YP realized that it needed to empower its advertisers (who they refer to as product owners). The company put them in full control of their own content, through the power of data analytics. By using sophisticated applications, which collect data on purchases and clicks, product owners can see how their customers are interacting with their online spaces. The range of services and information that YP is now able to offer its customers goes far beyond anything the company provided in the past, and is an excellent example of how a very traditional company re-imagined itself through the use of technology.

In order to achieve the kind of transformation that YP has undergone, it is important to have someone in your company scanning the marketplace to see what new tech tools are out there. Companies need to understand how to utilize and mobilize these technologies throughout their companies. The fact of the matter is, the companies that learn how to do this will thrive.

The first step in this process involves asking three questions.

1. **How is technology impacting your industry?** How can these tools be embedded into your business cycles? You need to have someone constantly scanning the market to see which tools are out there. Someone else should be working to streamline order fulfillment — to find a technology that can help make you better, faster, or provide the greatest possible customer experience.

2. **How does the technology impact your customers?** How are customers using technology? What are they using to connect to service providers? How are they gathering information? What kind of technology can be leverage for billing or service fulfillment?

3. **How does technology impact the way you work?** To answer this question it is necessary to turn your gaze within the company to see what kind of new collaboration tools are out there. How are people using technology to be more efficient, productive, creative, and to work with virtual teams?

## ASSESSING

Questioning and critiquing your operations and the range and value of your products and services is good and necessary, but it is crucial to ensure that you are asking the *right* questions. Are you trying to cast too wide a net? Are you overcomplicating what you are doing?

The answers may be surprising.

Sometimes important and necessary change may not involve going in a new direction; instead, it may involve going back to basics, simplifying things. This is true for people, and it can be true for businesses, too. In some cases, the best way forward, the best kind of change, involves returning to one's roots, focusing on what one does best. This is why a number of companies are streamlining and focusing on their core competencies. Simplifying things has allowed these companies to do what they do really well.

"Companies should never stay still," Steve Forbes told me. "It's important to maintain a healthy anxiety — to keep learning and keep trying to find ways to get stronger. Businesses that do so will be better able to compete."

Getting answers, whatever they are, isn't easy. Indeed, going through the process and exercise of asking these questions can be overwhelming. However, it's an essential step if you truly want to understand your market and its audience.

What's important to remember, too, is that because the world is constantly changing, a savvy business leader needs to be constantly recalibrating the equations that govern the marketplace. There are fewer and fewer "constants" in the formula. The landscape keeps changing; consumers' habits and preferences — their loyalties — shift and evolve by the hour. Whatever technology dominated when you went to bed will have been made obsolete by the time you wake up. We keep finding ourselves facing new and unexpected challenges. And always new and more difficult questions.

Then why do so many of us rely on the same stock answers? It's a brave new world out there!

Your main focus should be, of course, your customers. You need to understand what they want, what's important to them, what isn't, what influences them, what doesn't, how they shop,. There are other questions, too. How do they work? How could this information impact your company? Does it? The answers will help drive all kinds of behaviour — how you communicate, the language, tone, and branding elements you use to create connections — and will help determine how you design and promote your products and services.

These questions are essential to ask yourself while exploring relevance. Questioning your relevance is the gateway to innovation. It reveals what you need to do differently, it uncovers if you need to bring new products to market or make adjustments, and quickly identifies what is and is not working. These insights will guide your innovation efforts which can then be unleashed by your intrapreneurs.

## CONTEXT

Relevance, of course, depends on context. What is relevant to one group of customers may not be relevant to another. The needs and wants of a teen are not the same as those of a senior; much of what appeals to women won't appeal to men. Context is key.

Without knowledge of your target market, without knowledge of consumer context, you cannot intelligently develop products or market them — you don't have the full picture. So, before making any big decisions on product development and marketing, step back and assess the *consumption context*. You wouldn't expect a plane to fly with only one wing, right? Make sure your project is fit to fly. Otherwise, failure is pretty much inevitable.

A good example of catering to context is evidenced in the contrasting success stories of Home Depot and IKEA in the Chinese market.

Home Depot is a warehouse-style dream-come-true retailer for the DIY (do-it-yourself) handyperson, and the chain has an enormous presence throughout North America. Well, it wasn't long before executives at Home Depot reviewed its domestic success and wondered why the same concept that was so successful in North America wouldn't be just as successful in one of the world's largest emergent consumer populations: China. Indeed, why not?

Well, timing is everything.

It just so happened that at the same time that Home Depot was dreaming of a new DIY empire in the East, the Chinese economy entered a dramatic growth spurt. A new and vibrant middle class was anxious to show off its wealth and to enjoy the thrill of conspicuous consumption after years of government control and restrictions. Unfortunately for Home Depot, it turns out that among this class of *nouveau riche* spenders, no one *wanted* to do it themselves.

DIY is popular in wealthy Western countries with large and successful middle classes, but for people in developing countries it was taken as a stigma of poverty. Only poor people were forced to build their own homes.

IKEA, on the other hand, has been doing extremely well in China. Why?

The answer lies in the very different shopping experience found in IKEA stores, compared to that of Home Depot. IKEA does an excellent job with its floor displays. Customers who walk in don't have to imagine how the furnishings and accessories the company sells will look in their homes; the store is filled with sets that beautifully showcase the company's products. IKEA showrooms are immersive experiences. Customers can see how the products look in a room and say, "Yes, I want this." Once the decision to buy has been made, the customers just have to take their purchases home. They can then assemble the furniture themselves — something that is quite easy to do with IKEA's products — or pay to have someone do it for them. This is important to Chinese consumers.

The shopping experiences provided by Home Depot and IKEA are very different. Both are very successful businesses, but in the Chinese context, IKEA's business model is more attractive. Had Home Depot done more research on the Chinese market and the preferences of customers there — what their hobbies are, what is important to them — perhaps the company could have come up with another approach for the market, one that could have been more successful.

In order to fully understand context, I would encourage you to do the following, which actually takes us back to earlier chapters:

- **Don't make assumptions.** Just because something has worked in one context, doesn't mean it will work in another. Get the facts.
- **Ask questions and do your research.** Asking questions — as the Greek philosopher Socrates famously demonstrated — is the surest path to truth (in our case, meaningful breakthroughs). Once you do this, you will be able to better understand context.
- **Listen more and talk less.** Listening is probably the most ignored form of information acquisition. Few of us know how to listen productively and creatively, however. We are hardwired to respond.

Often the smartest and most productive approach is to *reflect* more and *react* less. Listening to other people and their ideas — figuring out *where* their ideas are coming from and *what* their perspectives are — helps orient and broaden your own thinking and perspectives. Creative thinking and problem solving is all about learning how to think from as many different perspectives as possible. That will never happen if the *only* voice you ever hear is your own.

Understanding what is going on at a macro level and identifying the things you need to know or understand at a sublevel are very important. Find that out, and work from there. Context is queen.

# CHAPTER EIGHT

## Creativity

IN THE 1960s, scientific researchers George Land and Beth Jarman devised a creativity test for NASA, to aid in the selection of innovative scientists and engineers. NASA considered the study to be a success for their purposes, but the scientists were left wanting more information about creativity and where it comes from. Are people born with creativity? Or, is it learned?

The Land and Jarman creativity test studied the subjects' ability to think of innovative solutions to problems. They administered their test to 1,600 five-year-old children. Incredibly, ninety-eight percent of those children were deemed "highly creative."

The scientists re-tested each subject five years later. In the second test, only thirty percent of these same children scored in the same range. When tested at the age of fifteen, the number deemed highly creative had dropped to twelve percent.

When 280,000 adults were given the same test, only two percent tested as highly creative.

Based on these results, Land and Jarman determined that "non-creative behaviour is learned."

\* \* \*

Creativity is one of the core attributes of intrapreneurs. They continually strive to imagine and re-imagine a better world.

It isn't that adults lack creativity. We all have the creative gene hard-wired in our brains. The problem is that, like any muscle, it has to be stretched and exercised daily or it will shrink and atrophy. An important goal of the greenhouse approach is learning how to exercise the creative muscles we all have.

## THE VITAL INGREDIENT

If creativity is an essential quality of our humanity, the question is, is it important for businesses and companies? Most people associate creativity with the work of artists and designers, but the truth is, creativity is crucial in all aspects of life — especially business. Creative thinking is essential in the business world. Look at it this way: you may not have the skills to paint a *Mona Lisa*, but you probably have more than enough creative appreciation for it as a work of art. Its beauty and craftsmanship engages you at a deeper and more emotional level (I hope!) than a quarterly report or monthly sales summary might. We all have it, okay; what we need to do is trust it. And that takes some creative-thinking rewiring.

A creative person will look at problems and situations and be able to consider them from a fresh perspective, a perspective that suggests unorthodox solutions. As we have seen, intrapreneurs are thinkers who dissect, reverse-engineer, and re-imagine ideas and concepts, procedures and processes, and products and markets. Creative thinking empowers people to look at a problem or situation from a new perspective, using imagination and curiosity to evaluate the issue at hand. It fosters the ability to make connections between things that may not seem to correlate and to find interesting points of intersection.

Even if you are not a designer or artist, you can still be a creative thinker. Regardless of the discipline you're in — human resources, operations, finance — we're all in the business of solving problems. And how do we solve problems? By applying creative thinking. Almost everything we do involves some element of design and creativity.

A fascinating study was commissioned by Adobe and Forrester Consulting in 2014 to assess how creativity influences business outcomes.* Senior managers from a broad sample of industries were surveyed to qualify and quantify the types of impacts creativity has on business results. Companies in which a culture of creativity is embraced, the report concluded, outperform on key business indicators such as market share, talent acquisition, and revenue growth.

It should come as no surprise that businesses practising creativity are more innovative than those that are not. When creative thinking is encouraged in a company, either through brainstorming informally or as part of a more structured process, the company will surpass its competitors.

For businesses to survive throughout the next industrial revolution (4IR — Fourth Industrial Revolution)** and beyond, they must stay ahead of their competitors. Both relevance and creative thinking will be required to do this. Both of these qualities are core to intrapreneurship.

Knowledge alone won't generate innovative ideas. You need creative thinking as well. Even when innovations are envisaged, creative thinking is required to refine those innovations until they're just right. The greater your curiosity and depth of knowledge, the more combinations of ideas you can come up with, the more innovative you can be.

Neil Blumenthal is co-founder and co-CEO of Warby Parker, an eyeglass company that specializes in offering affordable alternatives to expensive eyewear. Warby Parker not only offers designer eyewear at a reasonable price, but the company is socially responsible. For every pair of eyeglasses purchased, a pair is donated to those in need.

Creativity and social responsibility is the essence of Warby Parker's entire business ethos. The central motto of the firm, according to Blumenthal, is "learn, grow, repeat." Warby Parker encourages its employees to engage as much as possible with social causes and community initiatives; for instance, it offers a fully stocked free lending library for employees, regular skills training, and internal conventions. But Warby Parker also asks staff members for their creative ideas. Every week, employees submit their innovative ideas, which keeps everyone in a creative mindset.

---

* Forrester Consulting, "The Creative Dividend: How Creativity Impacts Business Results" (Forrester Consulting, 2014), landing.adobe.com/dam/downloads/whitepapers/55563. en.creative-dividends.pdf.

** Klaus Schwab, *The Fourth Industrial Revolution* (New York: Crown Publishing Group, 2016).

"Creativity is a business imperative," Blumenthal says.

Creative thinkers are the dreamers of the world. They are the people who pose questions like "What if?" Creative people have been classified as happier and generally more open-minded than other people, and the good news is that almost everyone has the potential to be creative.

# CHAPTER NINE

## Speed

REMEMBER THE FOLK TALE about the tortoise and the hare?

Forget about it. Trust me. Fast beats slow *every time*. It's a fundamental truth. And nowhere is timing more important than in business. Speed is key to success. Intrapreneurs, the dedicated, purposeful teams in a business, can cut through the corporate layers that can often slow big companies down.

## FAST FASHION: FROM RUNWAY TO STORE

Traditionally, fashion designers release their hot new lines on the runway six months before the clothes hit retail stores. Most high-end designers release two lines each year.

Amancio Ortega, owner and founder of Spanish clothing retailer Zara, looked at this way of doing business and saw an opportunity. "Why should consumers have to wait so long before they get these new styles?" he asked himself. Styles come and go, and Ortega knew that the company that brought a new line to the stores first would have a competitive advantage. He looked at clothing as being a perishable commodity, like milk or bread.

Zara created a new phenomenon, known as "fast fashion." Ortega's global brand produces high-fashion designs, in limited supply, at a low cost. It operates on a two-week cycle, with garments being "freshly baked" (designed) and distributed to retail stores in only fifteen days. From runway to store in two weeks? It was unheard of!

Until it wasn't.

Zara produces a finite run of each item, which appeals to the desire of the consumer to have exclusive items. If you go to the store too late, you may miss out entirely on a hot new item.

In order for this "fast-fashion" formula to work, Zara depends on speed in every part of its supply chain. Distributors, warehouse managers, buyers, subcontractors, production staff, designers, market specialists, store managers … everyone must be lightning quick in their part of the supply chain for this model to be successful. And successful it is. Zara is one of the most lucrative retail stores in the world.

Not only has Zara conquered speed, but it's staying ahead of the curve by leveraging new technology. An exemplar of a company that exploits the third industrial revolution, Zara is already using augmented reality. In select stores, customers can hold up their phones and see models in Zara designs come to life on their screens; they can simply shop the look and buy the design on the spot.

The H&M business model, by way of contrast, is about mass production and high volume. Everyone wants trendy clothes, right? What H&M pioneered very successfully was mass-market couture knock-offs: runway fashions at a fraction of the cost. Unfortunately, after years of success, sales began to plummet and H&M is closing stores and watching market share disappear.*

One school of thought blames H&M's downturn on poor e-commerce sales. But is this true? What seems more likely is that H&M has not taken the time to understand its customers. I'm not a retail expert, but I do know that fashion is the way people express their individuality. Zara saw that, and it created an entire model around limited quantity designs and exclusivity. People choose clothes to express their self-identity and uniqueness. This is the insight that Zara understands, that it has found a way to capitalize on. By offering limited supplies of attractive clothes, Zara allows people the opportunity to become part of an exclusive club

---

* Elizabeth Segran, "Is Fast Fashion Dying? H&M Shutters Stores as Sales Decline," Fast Company (January 2018), fastcompany.com/40525437/is-fast-fashion-dying-hm-shutters-stores-as-sales-decline.

— at a reasonable price. This is something that other retailers, producing mass volume of clothes, didn't understand in time. As a result, they've missed the ball.

Zara is remaining relevant, creatively embracing new technology, and doing it with speed; all fundamentals to intrapreneurship. H&M is struggling with technology, is too large to move with speed, and, in my opinion, is failing to remain relevant.

Zara's hip introduction of smartphone technology, using holographic images, was only one innovation. Zara is also looking at new ways to use technology to tap into the psyche of their customer base. By enabling customers to create virtual visions of themselves in its clothes, Zara enables the sharing of the shopping experiences in its stores on social media. Customers can get opinions and input from their friends and family, and those people can see what's on offer in Zara stores. A super smart initiative.

\* \* \*

We opened *The Greenhouse Approach* with the idea that we are living in a nanosecond culture. Faster and faster. Bring your product to market before anyone else or risk falling to the back of the pack. It's all about novelty. It's all about the next "big thing." And what is all that junk in the dumpster out back behind your warehouse? Exactly: *yesterday's* next big thing. Do you think I am exaggerating?

More and more, products are hitting the market in ever-faster cycles and customers are being trained to raise their expectations, making speed-to-market even more important.

Fast might beat slow, but done also beats perfect.

Having a good idea is one thing, believing in the ideas enough to let them go is another.

## TECHNOLOGY AND DATA

Relevance and creativity are crucial qualities for a successful business. In today's market, however, you must also be guided by speed.

Speed-to-market is a popular business mantra, but it's a concept that businesses struggle to maximize. This is primarily due to four failures:

complex and outdated processes, old technology, talent shortages, and the inability to intelligently use data.

How can those problems be fixed? By creatively embracing and utilizing new technologies and allowing the creativity of the intrapreneurs in your company to imagine and execute solutions.

Everything is dependent on good technology or a reliable system. If your company isn't moving quickly and keeping ahead of technological changes, your innovation process will suffer as a result. It is really about using technology and data in the right way. If you're collecting information on buying patterns and consumer habits, you need to take that data, analyze it, and incorporate the findings into your next production run. Data is the new currency. If you don't take meaningful data and use it, it is simply wasted.

Zara is a great example of a successful company that embodies the embrace-and-exploit enthusiasm for creative marketing made possible with the newest technology (especially as related to social media). Innovation and opportunity are mutually inclusive. One begets the other.

Your competitors are investing in innovation, but there's a chance you can beat them to market if you can innovate with speed, applying your data and information.

# CHAPTER TEN

## Clarity

I STARTED WORKING at TELUS when it was still a telecommunications company. TELUS soon embarked on a transformational journey during which it grew and changed dramatically through a series of mergers and acquisitions. Within five years, the company made some strategic acquisitions to achieve its goal of being an integrated communications technology company.

By the end of this process, TELUS was offering over eight hundred products and services. Its growth had been spectacular and its market reach was enviable. Unfortunately, it was also unclear to a lot of consumers exactly who TELUS was or what they did. Even the employees were confused. There were way too many different branches on the tree. Too many marquees on the same storefront.

Generally speaking, growth in business is a good thing. It means you and the company are doing things right. Consumers know who you are and like your product. What is not good is growth minus clarity. And the ticklish problem about clarity is that — also generally speaking — a company doesn't know it has lost its clarity until it's too late.

Remember our story about Microsoft? Right. TELUS found itself in the same predicament. The company had to retrace its steps and bring back its focus. Remember the North Star we talked about earlier? When you're out in your car and you realize you are lost, what is the first thing you do?

Well, unless you are the average male driver, you consult a map. You know where you want to go, but you have wandered off course. Businesses need to do exactly the same thing.

What did TELUS do? It knew it had to reorganize the business. Fundamental to that was the process of answering a number of questions.

- Which of the company's eight hundred products and services complemented each other?
- Which ones were similar?
- How could the company categorize and consolidate them?
- What language and terminology was necessary to ensure that current and potential customers understood the qualities and value of what was being offered?

TELUS went through the process of rethinking, consolidating, and simplifying itself. It organized its products and services into six "solution sets" — each set offered products and services to provide a solution to a customer need. This process allowed the company to clearly articulate what it was in the business of doing. At that point, a clear and concise mission statement was created for each set, something that communicated what each set offered, the features of each product and service, and how they could be combined to provide added value.

TELUS was then able to craft a statement for its customers and employees that clearly identified the company's mission, and how each of its solution sets and their constituent products and services contributed to successfully satisfying its customers' needs. Everything was built around these solution sets: sales training, customer training, and marketing campaigns. Everyone at this point knew what we were in the business of doing, and understood the importance and power of clarity.

* * *

To get what you want, in business and in life, you must be clear about what it is you're after. What is your *goal*? What is it that you want to achieve? Without clarity, without focus, you will be unable to identify your goals and, therefore, your needs and wishes. Your thoughts and ideas will be muddled. If things are not clear to you, how will you be able to make them clear to anyone else? I've always been told that if you can't explain something, then you don't understand it.

One of the core competencies common to the intrapreneur is the ability to simplify complex problems. An intrapreneur has the ability to distill ideas and concepts to reveal what is important.

Clarity is required at all levels of a company, but it's an especially important quality for managers to have. All forms of direction, written and spoken, need a clear focus. What is the subject of the message? Is there a problem? What is the solution? If it doesn't seem to exist, what can be done to identify one? The team members need to fully comprehend what is expected of them — how they can best communicate and what they are encouraged to do and not to do.

When your company lacks clarity of focus, organization productivity and innovation will suffer and you will find it hard to hold onto talent. Again, it all comes down to creating the environment where creativity can flourish. Your people need to know you want them to be creative and that you want them to help you to remain relevant by thinking laterally, bringing their ideas to you, and standing up for their beliefs. If you hire the right people, they will make your company successful; but you must make it clear to them what you expect.

## FOSTERING CLARITY

Confused people are unproductive people. When you're clear about the goals, and the strategy to achieve those goals is made explicit, it will unleash the productivity needed to succeed. If team members constantly are wondering, "What are we supposed to be doing right now?" how can they be productive?

As a leader, you must clearly communicate what the mandate of the company is, and what people are required to do.

- What is required by their function or role?
- What are their deliverables?
- What do they need to get done?

A job description is just a guide. Leaders need to constantly monitor, decide if changes need to be made, and communicate to workers what their priorities should be. Let them know if alterations need to be made to procedures and practices.

The marketplace is constantly changing, and to remain relevant, companies need to change. Managing change is difficult, though. The successful company will assess what needs to be altered to continue to meet its goals, and how best to execute whatever changes need to be made. Fundamental to that is clearly communicating revised goals to employees. Otherwise, they will become confused about what is expected of them. Again, when people are confused, they are unproductive.

Are your teams clear about what work they are supposed to achieve? Because it's possible that your understanding of what they should be doing is different from theirs, it's up to you to close the gap by providing clarity at three core levels: company, team, and individual.

- **Company**. Leaders must be clear about the visions, mandates, and goals of the company. In my interview with Raja Rajamannar, he said that his role as a leader is to articulate his vision clearly, and then ensure that his team has the necessary tools to make that vision a reality — an even more perfect reality if that vision can be improved.
- **Team**. What are your groups and teams responsible for? Does the organization of these teams support the goals of the company? Teams need to be linked to the overall mandate and goals of a company or a specific project in order for them to be able to work together toward a common outcome.
- **Individual**. Not only must companies and their teams be clear about their focus, the individual employees must also be perfectly clear about what is expected of them. In fact, employees' understanding of their company's and team's focus is essential for the success of a company. Simply stated, your workers must understand the focus of the company and their team, and they must also understand what their function is within the context of those larger wholes.

If your company's focus is blurry or imprecise, productivity will be working negatively and at cross-purposes. Teams must work together to fulfill the goals of the company, and individuals must work together to fulfill the needs of their teams. It is a hand-in-glove type of scenario. You must be clear on the specific tasks your individual employees need to complete.

Maintaining clarity is of great importance for companies, as it will determine how the flow of work will take place, which ultimately impacts the quantity and quality of output. As we all know, however, in any company — big or small — things can go sideways quickly. The need for clear and authentic communication will become the cultural fabric and, like a muscle, the more you flex it, the stronger it will become.

# CHAPTER ELEVEN

## Accountability

As we learned earlier, gone are the days of 9-to-5. For many of us, our work environment could literally be wherever we happen to be at that moment.

Technology has freed us from the yoke of the traditional office or workstation. Many of us can work wherever — even whenever — we need to. Smart company leaders are embracing a less traditional model and exploring opportunities for flexible work routines, always with an idea of maximizing productivity. Remember, a company needs to be in agreement about "what" it needs; where flexibility and creative adaptation comes in is with the "how."

Of course, while employees may no longer be spending as much time in the office, they still must meet deadlines and efficiency targets. When your teams are working from home, co-working spaces, or coffee shops, you must implement a process that will hold those employees accountable for their output and the work that they create.

Accountability — specifically, positive accountability — is my fifth guiding principle for today's business leaders.

The word "accountability" is often associated with "liability," a word that has negative connotations — legal liability is not something that most people embrace. Fear is embedded into this term. Some employees are afraid to be accountable. Why? Probably, they fear that if they are held accountable, they will be blamed for something not getting done. For these employees, accountability is seen as a negative thing, something to be avoided.

When something goes wrong, assigning accountability can be used as an excuse for punishment, a way of blaming someone for something. When that happens, the results are negative. Problems aren't acknowledged because people are afraid of being held accountable for them; as a result, lessons aren't learned, changes aren't made. Employees become afraid to come forward with new ideas, and become less productive overall. But, if accountability is equated with responsibility, companies will experience positive results. According to the United States Office of Personnel Management,* positive accountability leads to greater employee morale, impoved performance, greater employee involvement, and an increased commitment to work.

## EMPOWERMENT THROUGH RESPONSIBILITY

In my experience in the corporate world, I have always felt proud when my managers trusted me enough to be accountable for projects or initiatives, because it meant that they had faith in me — and for me that means a lot. The same is true for others. Employees who are made responsible and held accountable get things done — they will feel empowered, they will feel trusted.

One of the key attributes that intrapreneurs possess is the ability to know what they are accountable for. They are not afraid of owning items or responsibilities regardless of whether or not they flourish. They have this deep inner ability to feel complete comfort with accountability that allows them to drive projects forward.

Giving your employees responsibility and making them accountable for their work is a good thing for your business or company. But how do you manage your employees and the work on a day-to-day basis? Early in my career, I learned the power of project management. Project management is an incredibly effective tool for holding people accountable. It helps you to look at how and when work gets done. The company's work is divided into projects. Then the different aspects of each project are assigned measurable targets. What are the work packets, what are the milestones, the dependencies, the timing, and which people are accountable? This approach helps to

---

* United States Office of Personnel Management, "Accountability Can Have Positive Results," OPM.Gov, opm.gov/policy-data-oversight/performance-management/reference-materials/more-topics/accountability-can-have-positive-results/.

make sure that projects are done well and on time. And when things don't go well, this approach makes it easier to see what happened and why. Of course, discovering problems makes it easier to fix them.

Intrapreneurial-oriented project management is an approach that should be used much more widely in work and is fundamental to the greenhouse approach. It is a powerful tool.

\* \* \*

We have been discussing employee accountability, but I want to take a step back for a moment and look at accountability in a larger context. The accountability of the company. It's hard to expect employees to feel that they should be accountable for their work if the company that they work for does not strive to hold itself accountable to its employees and customers.

Patagonia is a company that sells outdoor clothing and gear. It is committed to conducting its business in a socially and environmentally constructive way. On its website, at The Footprint Chronicles, customers can find incredibly detailed information on its manufacturing and distribution process. It provides answers to such questions as "Where does Patagonia manufacture its products?" "Do workers in Patagonia factories make a living wage?" "How does Patagonia weigh its commitments to environmental versus social responsibility?" The foundational principles of the company's business approach are transparency and accountability. Every aspect of the company's operations — the choice of suppliers, the treatment of employees and the environment by those suppliers, etc. — are open for inspection by customers. There is no secrecy.

These discussions invite the consumer to be a part of the supply chain process, and the company welcomes feedback on how it can be improved. This very public view of sharing and openness engages their audience in meaningful ways that start to build trust and loyalty — an excellent example of the importance of a company being accountable at all levels.

Needless to say, the employees of Patagonia are very motivated and strive to ensure their work contributes to the success of the company. The commitment to accountability on the part of the company serves as a powerful motivator for the employees of Patagonia.

Patagonia has embraced accountability as a business model. It has gone far beyond the standard concept of "quality" that many companies advertise themselves as providing. Patagonia has re-imagined the term. If your company wants to re-imagine accountability, I think there are some easy ways to do that.

First, you need to define accountability for your company. In business management, we talk a lot about "dependencies." It's really very simple. None of us operate in a void; what I do in my job invariably impacts what and how you do your job. Employees need to understand what those dependencies are and what they mean in terms of performance and productivity — to hitting the target or reaching the goal. Let team members know that people are depending on them to get their work done. It is vitally important that the conversation evolves from "I" to "we." It's about keeping the team engaged. If one person doesn't complete a task, it will impact the whole team and the team's commitments.

One of the things that people and companies need to be aware of is that when one person is allowed to miss a commitment, it creates a snowball effect, a culture of tolerance for this kind of behaviour. This leads to a poor work ethic. Employees need to be held accountable for their work. However, accountability should not be primarily a negative thing; it should be positive. It should be equated with responsibility. When employees are given responsibility, when they are given the power to make meaningful decisions, the results will be positive. Assigning your employees responsibility — accountability — for a task and then allowing them to operate as freely as possible to achieve that task, is the best way to engage talent to meet performance and productivity goals and benchmarks.

The greenhouse approach is all about nurturing talent. It will take time and effort. Healthy and receptive soil does not prepare itself. The greenhouse approach should be intrinsic to how your company works. The model that I have developed helps ensure that it becomes habitual.

# CHAPTER TWELVE

## Experimentation

**THE GREATEST INNOVATORS** of our time planned experiments deliberately, as they were on a path to discovery.

## DELIBERATE DISCOVERY

### Galileo Galilei

Legend has it that Galileo dropped two balls, one heavy and one light, from a tower in Pisa. Contrary to conventional wisdom, the story goes, the two balls landed at the same time. So much for conventional wisdom, right?

But the actual experiment he used was much better.

The Italian inventor carved a groove down the centre of a board about twenty feet long by ten inches wide. He propped the board at an angle and timed how quickly two balls rolled down the track. He discovered that the weight of the ball had no relationship to the distance that the balls travelled. Rather, the distance the balls travelled was proportional to the square of the time that elapsed.

How, in an age before clocks, could Galileo measure this so precisely?

Historians believe he used music.

Along the ball's path, Galileo placed catgut frets, like those used on a lute. As the rolling ball clicked against the frets, he sang a tune, using the upbeats to time the motion, effectively discovering a new law of gravity.

## William Harvey

Harvey was dubious of the Greek physician Galen's classic anatomy teachings, which said the body contains two separate vascular systems: a blue "vegetative" fluid, the elixir of nourishment and growth, which flowed through veins; and the bright red "vital" fluid, which travelled through the arteries, activating muscles and stimulating motion. Galen taught that invisible spirits, or "pneuma," caused the fluids to slosh back and forth like the tides. The heart just went along for the ride, expanding and contracting like a bellows.

Harvey cut open a snake and used forceps to pinch the main vein (vena cava) just before it entered the heart. The space downstream from the obstruction emptied of blood, while the heart grew paler and smaller, as though it were about to die. When Harvey released the grip, the heart refilled and sprung back to life.

Pinching the heart's main artery had the opposite effect. The space between the heart and forceps engorged with blood, inflating like a balloon. It was the heart, not invisible spirits, that was the driving motor, pushing red, oxygenated blood to the extremities of the body, where it passed into the bluish veins and returned to the heart, for rejuvenation.

Harvey deduced that there was only one kind of blood and it moved in a circle. It circulated.

## Ivan Pavlov

Contrary to popular belief, Pavlov hardly ever used bells in his experiments with salivating dogs. His animals were more discriminating. In the "Tower of Silence," sealed from distractions, dogs were taught to distinguish between objects rotating clockwise and counter-clockwise, between a circle and an ellipse, even between subtle shades of grey. But, for his most remarkable experiment, Pavlov used music.

First, a dog was trained to salivate when it heard an ascending scale, but no reaction was encouraged for a descending one. What, Pavlov wondered, would happen if the animal listened to other combinations of the same notes? The melodies were played and the spittle collected.

Through simple conditioning, the dog had categorized the music it heard into two groups, depending on whether the pitches were predominantly rising or falling.

The mind had lost a bit of its mystery. Pavlov had shown how learning was a matter of creatures forming new connections in a living machine.

## Robert Millikan

By bending a cathode ray with an electrical field, Cambridge scholar J.J. Thomson had shown electricity to be a form of matter, and measured the ratio of its charge to its mass. It followed that electricity was made of particles, but to clinch the case, someone needed to isolate and measure one.

In Robert Millikan's Chicago laboratory, two round brass plates, the top one with a hole drilled through the centre, were mounted on a stand and illuminated from the side by a bright light. The plates were then connected to a thousand-volt battery.

With a perfume atomizer, Millikan sprayed a mist of oil above the apparatus and watched through a telescope as some of the droplets (they looked like little stars) fell into the area between the plates.

As he tweaked the voltage, he watched as some drops were pushed slowly upward while others were pulled down. Their passage through the atomizer had ionized them, giving the drops negative or positive charges.

By timing their movement with a stopwatch, Millikan showed that charge, like pocket change, came in discrete quantities. He had found the electron.

\* \* \*

What can we learn from the above examples? Many of the greatest discoveries were the product of planned experimentation. Hypotheses were created, experiments were designed, results were analyzed — and then, if necessary, hypotheses were refined, and processes were adjusted. All of this is true. But some of the greatest innovations of our time have not been planned; they have been accidental, such as penicillin and Post-it Notes. None of these discoveries were the result of planned, deliberate innovation.

Experimentation has been fundamental to scientific progress since ancient times. It remains so today. Virtually all of the products and services that we enjoy in the modern world are products of experimentation. In fact, the amazing quality of life most of us enjoy today and take for granted is the result of experimentation. Testing of ideas, experimentation, and innovation are also fundamental to business success. The companies that succeed are those that embrace progress, that have embedded experimentation in their corporate culture.

We exist in an age of disruption. Managers know this, but many don't apply the fundamental idea of experimentation to their company's work environments. Why?

Many managers, involved in the day-to-day struggle to operate their companies, will tell you that business needs to happen and so there is little time (or not enough resources) left to experiment. My model addresses this quandary. It forces people to think differently and approach each problem from an inventor's mindset. This model forces people to think with a "What if?" approach.

## THE INVENTOR'S MINDSET

Good experimental thinking has been said to be divergent, something that takes you away from the obvious path ... in the very best of ways. Experimental thinking is a process of discovery and learning. This means that you will fail. I often speak about the idea of "fail fast, recover fast" in my talks. Learn from your mistake and move on. The goal has not changed.

The success of a company like Amazon has been attributed to its emphasis on experimentation. According to Jeff Bezos, the CEO of Amazon, "Our success . . . is a function of how many experiments we do per year, per month, per week, per day. We've tried to reduce the cost of doing experiments so that we can do more of them."

Experimenting can lead to great success, but there will, of course, be failures, too. It's necessary to keep that in mind. In today's work environments, we hear very little about the failures, the experiments that didn't immediately result in success or great discoveries. We only hear about winners. Angry Birds, for instance, the spectacularly successful online game franchise, was anything but an overnight success. Rovio, the company that developed Angry Birds, failed fifty-one times before it hit pay dirt. It wasn't getting it wrong that motivated Rovio, of course, but getting it right.

Bill Gates is enormously successful, but he, too, has suffered his share of failures. He often refers to his first company, Traf-O-Data, as the founding of Microsoft. The company had developed a software tool for analyzing traffic data, which was of use to traffic engineers. It was a good idea, but it had a flawed business model. Gates's experience in developing and marketing Traf-O-Data, despite the company's failure, taught him a number of important lessons, and played a crucial role in the formation and success of Microsoft. The lesson learned was a key step in creating Microsoft.

Bezos has gone on record discussing the relationship between success and failure:

> Given a 10 percent chance of a one-hundred-times payoff, you should take that bet every time. But you're still going to be wrong nine times out of ten. We all know that if you swing for the fences, you're going to strike out a lot, but you're also going to hit some home runs. The difference between baseball and business, however, is that baseball has a truncated outcome distribution. When you swing, no matter how well you connect with the ball, the most runs you can get is four. In business, every once in a while, when you step up to the plate, you can score 1,000 runs. This long-tailed distribution of returns is why it's important to be bold. Big winners pay for so many experiments.[*]

Since discovery and learning are part of good experimentation, good experimentation will result in many failures, but you'll also learn a lot.

Experimentation that results in failure is viewed unfavourably by most companies. No Six Sigma–certified firm tolerates "lots of failures" for long. Too often experimenting looks like "non-value added" work, which should be eliminated.

Of course, the cost of experimentation can be high, but there are ways to minimize the cost and maximize the benefits. Amazon is an example of a company that has figured out how to reduce the cost of conducting experiments so that they can do more of them. Amazon Prime, Kindle, and Echo were all experiments. So was Amazon Web Service (AWS), which is Amazon's cloud computing service, and it is now worth billions.

---

* Eugene Kim, "The Best Business Advice from Jeff Bezos," Business Insider (April 21, 2016), businessinsider.com/business-advice-from-amazon-ceo-jeff-bezos-2016-4#-1.

\* \* \*

I have always been an experimenter. Early on I learned that it is through the process of experimentation that we discover things. This is such a simple truth. When I entered the working world I realized that, while experimentation is both necessary and valuable for success, you must be somewhat circumspect when advocating for the testing of new ideas and protocols. When I have taken this behaviour to the workplace, I have treaded carefully, knowing that there would be mistakes and that I would be accountable for the implications. That never deterred me from experimenting; it just forced me to do it more carefully, using a better-thought-out process.

Even when caution is employed, many companies are still fearful of change, of experimentation. In many corporations, outside of their research and development teams, experimentation is a dangerous word. Experimenting is often seen as a thoughtless approach to business, a kind of "winging it," rather than a considered attempt to obtain insight and knowledge. In such environments, where everything must be perfect the first time, experimentation loses and sameness wins.

In order to fight this mentality, to champion experimentation in your company, it is necessary to explain how it works and what its benefits are. It is necessary to make clear that experimentation is good, and even that failure is good. It must be made clear that it is through experimentation that we learn.

## RETHINKING EXPERIMENTATION TO HYPOTHESIS TESTING

A hypothesis is an explanation or theory that requires further investigation. What if we looked at experimentation as simply a broken-down series of hypotheses? Might this be easier to apply and institutionalize within a company?

This approach to experimentation would involve a step-by-step process to determine whether a stated theory or idea about a certain situation is true. This would lead to more innovation, while helping you deviate from assumptions by actively involving first principles thinking.

Hypothesis testing would enable you to make better-informed decisions about what to do moving forward or how to navigate around your options. This process, while enabling you to be freer with the ideas of risk and trial and error, can also present facts on projects or initiatives, revealing where you could be wasting time, capital, and resources.

Essentially, good hypotheses lead decision-makers to new and better ways of achieving business goals. When you need to make decisions, such as how much you should spend on advertising or what effect a price increase will have on your customer base, it's easy to make wild assumptions or get lost in analysis paralysis. A business hypothesis solves this problem because at the start it's based on some foundational information. In all of science, hypotheses are grounded in theory, as theory tells you what you can generally expect from a certain line of inquiry.

A hypothesis based on years of business research in a particular area, then, helps you focus, define, and appropriately direct your research. You won't go on a wild goose chase to prove or disprove it. A hypothesis predicts the relationship between two variables. If you want to study pricing and customer loyalty, you make a prediction statement so that you won't waste your time and resources studying tangential areas.

To form a good hypothesis, you should ensure certain criteria are met when making your prediction statements. Remember, some of your beliefs could be old assumptions, so look for current research.

The process could look like this.

- State the hypothesis. You have a theory to be tested, state it. Maybe there is a new feature in a product that you want to develop and you believe it will appeal to a particular audience.
- Collect some initial data and information that you believe could influence your hypothesis.
- Further refine your hypothesis based on the data and make some predictions on what you think will happen based on the information gathered.
- Test your hypothesis.
- Analyze the data and draw some conclusions and insights from the results.

This process rewires your thinking to come up with new ways of incorporating experimentation into your decision-making process. Better-informed decisions can be made.

# CHAPTER THIRTEEN

## Execution

Done is better than perfect.

— Sheryl Sandberg

**PEOPLE COME UP WITH** ideas all the time, but the hardest thing to do is to get people behind those ideas, and then to execute them.

Sandberg's idea that a launched product is more desirable than a better product that only exists theoretically is at the heart of the nanosecond business culture of our globalized economy. It's about having the gumption to just move with an idea before someone else does, or before it's too late.

Execution means knowing what needs to happen, when. What are the details that need to come together? Who is accountable for what?

When you start to shift gears in execution, reality kicks in, along with the fact that ideas are coming to fruition. I believe this is when fear often rears its ugly head. What if we're wrong?

This idea of realism, I believe, is what keeps us from moving forward with ideas … the fear that it may be the wrong path.

Simply ask yourself, is this project or idea going to be successful? Are we doing the right thing?

## PERFECTIONISM HINDERS EXECUTION

Remember: don't get stuck in the deep mud. Nothing needs to be perfect and nothing can ever be perfect. Perfection-pursuit paralysis is one of the biggest hindrances when it comes to execution.

After a keynote address in Cincinnati, an audience member came to speak to me. He said he was experiencing dissatisfaction at work. He had been with his company for five years and felt he hadn't accomplished anything. It's a shame. He was bright and energetic and he had wonderful ideas, but no one at his company was interested. What a waste! Human talent truly is our greatest and most irreplaceable resource and we waste it every single day.

Imagine what a manager or department head would say if they discovered that employees were making thousands of unnecessary document copies a month? Of course! The practice would be halted immediately. So why do we routinely ignore the waste of human talent? Isn't human ingenuity and problem solving worth at least as much as a case of copying paper?

The greenhouse approach is all about creating an environment in which intrapreneurship can flourish. Intrapreneurs always need to be moving forward, reaching farther. And that aspirational energy and goal-oriented mindset is *affective*; we want to breed an environment where enthusiastic and energetic people can operate and collaborate to produce great work. Conversely, a "different day, same task" environment easily becomes a business culture norm that is toxic to all.

So what does that have to do with perfection-pursuit paralysis? Just this: things need to get done. Innovation is key, but it is not enough: an innovation that works beautifully on the drawing board but can't make it past the first hurdle is a colossal waste of energy, time, and talent. Hurdles and roadblocks that restrain implementation need to be lowered. Does that mean that in the spirit of going faster and faster you take shortcuts and compromise on quality? No, never! Never compromise when it comes to quality. *A commitment to quality is non-negotiable.*

What we are talking about are myriad institutional and psychological barriers in a company that restrain goal-directed momentum. Water will run naturally down a slanted drainpipe. But if it hits a clog, it backs up, and that creates massive problems at both ends. Think of innovation as a clean pipe free of any restrictions. Ideas will flow through it like water.

Anxiety about perfection is a closed loop. It's one of the psychological barriers we create for ourselves to immunize us from regret. The greenhouse approach, however, is designed to minimize the opportunity for regret by creating systems that maximize performance — and always with an eye to quality-maintenance. Look, most of us would agree that if we are asked to do something in a rush, it increases the likelihood that we will make mistakes.

Remember that famous slogan spoken by Orson Welles many years ago: "We will sell no wine before its time!" Don't confuse speed, however, with increased performance. Asking a person to do the same redundant task over and over does increase the chances of a crash and burn. The idea is to speed things up by innovating: maybe there is a different way to perform the same task . . . only faster?

Take Instagram as an example.

According to experts, Instagram was not perfect when it was launched, but it was a strong enough product that it gained a huge amount of attention anyway. Instagram's developers continued to adapt Instagram's features and offerings as they went along. And as they did, they stuck to their one central concept — allowing people to share beautiful photographs using their mobile phones.

Within eighteen months of launching, Instagram was sold to Facebook for one billion dollars.

What might have happened had the developers waited until Instagram was perfect before launching? What if they got stuck in perfection paralysis?

Timing is everything, and done is better than perfect.

Here are some rules of thumb for execution.

- **Timing is key.** Because the world is moving so fast, timing is of the essence. If you don't move, someone else will, or your audience may lose interest. While the details are important, you cannot get bogged down in every little thing; you need to know when to move.
- **Being able to pivot is important.** When you are in the guts of a project and you realize something is not quite right, you may

need to change course. Often, when we are in execution mode, the thought of changing directions can be scary and some may be reluctant to do so. But being able to make changes and decisions quickly and efficiently while you are in operating mode is crucial.

- **Staying close.** Staying close and engaged when you are operating is very important. You need to be constantly monitoring and looking outside to see how things are resonating in the market, to know if changes need to be made, if modifications are necessary, or if you need to add any new resources, skills, etc.

You must have the ability to redirect during the execution phase. If something isn't working, you have to be able to pivot and change directions. Ride the wave, don't let it pull you under.

## BEFORE WE MOVE ON

In order for companies and businesses to be able to survive and thrive, they must be able to adapt during times of change. We're back to Darwin, okay? As business leaders, we must rethink change and see it for what it is — a constant force that we must work with and not against. We must be constantly observing and learning, ready to pivot and change with the tide instead of fighting against it. A sick or weak buffalo is dinner for the hungry lion. You don't want your company on the menu, do you?

Remember these four things as we navigate the next industrial revolution.

1. Be keenly aware of the current situation within your company.
2. Look closely at your products and services, and determine if they'll continue to serve your changing demographic or if adjustments must be made (my model will help you with this).
3. Re-imagine change and learn how to ride the wave.
4. Provide your teams with the knowledge and technology they will need to help your company be successful.

# THE SEVEN GUIDING PRINCIPLES: RECAP

Let the seven guiding principles be your North Star. Let's recap.

## 1. Relevance

Stay connected to your audiences. Tap into their psyche like Zara has done. Recruit trendspotters to help you see where your industry is going, and researchers to help you get there. Think about big brands like Sears, Blockbuster, and Sony. They all had one thing in common: they struggled to remain relevant in times of change. At this time, only one of those brands still exists. Will Sony be able to keep traction in the changing world of music? Time will tell.

## 2. Creativity

Scientists George Land and Beth Jarman proved that non-creative behaviour is learned. Their testing has shown that we lose our creativity as we grow older. But I believe that creative thinking is still within us. Creativity is one of the things that separates humans from machines. If humans want to remain relevant throughout the fourth industrial revolution in which AI and quantum computing are going to make much of our work irrelevant, we must harness our creative thinking powers and contribute our brilliance to the world of machines.

## 3. Speed

We live in a rapid-fire world when it comes to business. If you don't bring new products to market quickly, competitors will. Zara beautifully demonstrates the importance of speed when it comes to innovation. In fact, Zara has conquered this principle so well that it has changed the model upon which high fashion operates. It's difficult for large companies to be agile and to move quickly, but speed is a principle that must be embraced by all companies that wish to survive.

## 4. Clarity

To get what you want in business or in life, you have to be clear in your goals. Without clarity you will be unfocused and have trouble communicating your thoughts. You need to have company clarity,

clarity within your teams, and clarity with individuals. Clarity is a hand-in-glove thing. You must be clear on your goals and objectives and what you want individuals to be doing. Lack of clarity means your people are confused, and confused people are unproductive.

## 5. Accountability

You must re-imagine accountability and use it to empower your teams to do their best work. Help your teams understand that other people are depending on their work and that their work as individuals affects others. When teams have clarity, accountability is not difficult to achieve. Everyone should know exactly what their priorities and deliverables are and how their work feeds into other people's work to create output. If you are delayed, others will be delayed.

## 6. Experimentation

We've looked at how some of the best innovations and discoveries have been accidental, not the result of planned, deliberate experimentation. That teaches us that in business we should be open to the idea of experimenting. Perhaps when companies rethink the rules, there will be more time in the workday to be creative, to experiment, and to play. We learn from trial and error, and this should be a part of how we approach work.

## 7. Execution

We know that timing is everything in business, particularly in today's work environment. If we don't move quickly, an idea can become old, fast, and if you don't do it, someone else will. The important thing to keep in mind is that while you execute, it is good to pivot, to change direction if need be. If some aspect of your business isn't working, there might be another aspect that's doing extraordinarily well.

## HOW TO USE GUIDING PRINCIPLES

Guiding principles are philosophies, personal beliefs, and values that guide your company through all of its goals, thinking processes, and work. It is these principles that create cultural norms so that everyone understands what is important and how they should be approaching their work. These ideas will influence people and the decision-making process through all levels of the company. As indicated previously, all of these ideas are based on intrapreneurial mindsets and creating a culture of intrapreneurship. To create a credo for companies around these ideas, start with a simple question: "What if?" What if we shifted our thinking, our mindset, based on all of these ideas? What would the outcome be? What can it be?

* * *

These guiding principles will help you and your company to grow and to thrive. In the next section, I will discuss my model, which will help guide you through a variety of challenging, creative projects facing your company. The four phases of the model are: problem identification, ideation, execution, and reflection. Keeping these phases in mind, I will demonstrate how to work through applied learning and provide guidance for developing teams of intrapreneurs. This is where you'll see your greenhouse start to bloom.

PART THREE

# APPLYING THE MODEL

# CHAPTER FOURTEEN

## The Model — Making the Greenhouse Come Alive

THROUGHOUT *THE GREENHOUSE APPROACH* we have talked about the changes companies need to make in order to create a culture of intrapreneurship. Guiding principles need to be clarified; corporate structures and processes need to evolve. In this part of the book, I will show you, via a clear and simple model, how you can bring intrapreneurship to life within your workplace.

Ideas, even the greatest ones, will not be of any use to your company unless they are executed. And we must execute our ideas flawlessly. Flawless execution is not execution without mistakes. It is important to understand that when you and your team are executing an idea, things may go wrong. You need to incorporate the possibility of errors occurring into your plans. The important thing is to build backup strategies for what to do, how to quickly pivot if you need to, into your execution plans. If things do go sideways, you need to keep going, making corrections along the way.

To keep going despite setbacks, it is necessary to think through all of the necessary steps involved. Detailed questions need to be answered. To succeed, your company needs to both foster the creation of new solutions for the problems your company faces and execute those breakthrough ideas. My model presents four key phases that need to be followed from idea inception to implementation. But first, we need to discover why a large number of companies struggle with this task.

# REASONS FOR FAILURE

My research shows that companies often fail to foster new ideas and execute those ideas. There are three main reasons for this failure: diplomacy, complacency, and inward focus.

## Diplomacy

Diplomacy is defined as "the art of dealing with people in a sensitive and effective way." Most people have a positive view of diplomacy. They see it as helpful in solving problems. Actually, diplomacy gets in the way. In my interview with Steve Forbes, he said, "People are afraid to disagree at work in fear of offending their friends."

When you are diplomatic, in other words, change doesn't happen.

The Dutch believe that there is great benefit to be had in "speakability," or being direct. Straightforwardness is so intrinsic in Dutch society that there's a special word for it: *bespreekbaarheid*. When you are in a meeting in the Netherlands and you say something that isn't very smart, it will be pointed out. Nobody is going to pretend that what you've said is interesting or useful just to spare your feelings. The Dutch believe that everything can and should be talked about.

Such candour is rare in most companies, however. As a result, there is no clear direction. When leaders fail to inspire their employees to work toward a common goal, each team will tend to veer off in its own direction. It becomes impossible to integrate all the silos.

## Complacency

Successful companies can become complacent when they feel that their size and domination in the marketplace rules. They feel they are untouchable and the thought of change scares them. To them, the amount of work and effort involved in changing outweighs the cost of just keeping things as they are. This is a dangerous attitude to have during turbulent business times.

To combat complacency, companies need to ignite a culture of curiosity within them. Curiosity, as I've mentioned before, is one of the greatest gifts one can possess. A curious mind will always question things.

Employees need to be encouraged to question if a company's products and services are still relevant, if they can be improved. The way a company does business needs to be questioned. Its structures should be reviewed. Everything should be on the table. Encouraging curiosity and combating complacency is the best way for a company to ensure its continuing success.

### Inward Focus

Too often, companies focus so much attention on internal problems and office politics that they can't seem to move — they get caught up in the day-to-day concerns. Attention must be paid to the running of a company, of course, but this focus should never come at the expense of looking at what is going on in the marketplace.

I have said over and over that companies need to be constantly assessing the market, to ensure that what they are selling is still relevant to customers. Companies that spend too much time and attention trying to get "buy in" from their own team members risk losing sight of what's going on in the market. The primary focus of any company's activities should always be satisfying its customers' needs and wants, today and in the future. Keeping both in mind is crucial for the continuing success of any company.

* * *

These three problems are common to the culture in many companies. I've suggested ways of doing things, patterns of thought that should be avoided, and alternatives that should be aimed for. It all sounds simple, right? Not really. The reality is that creating meaningful change is often very difficult. And, of course, time and money are always issues. So, what's the solution?

## PROBLEM SOLVING

The most important thing needed to properly implement an idea is a clear understanding of what the problems are. Until the exact nature of a problem has been clearly articulated, it's not possible to solve the problem, to improve the situation.

Companies too often start projects and initiatives without clearly thinking about why they are doing the work that they are doing. They don't take the time to think about it. This requires rigour and discipline, time and effort. I have seen and experienced the wrong problems being worked on in companies, or cases where no one took the time to dig deeper into what those problems were.

The importance of laying the proper groundwork before attempting to solve a problem is emphasized in a popular statement that is generally attributed to the scientific luminary Albert Einstein, "You need a strong foundation before you lay the bricks of a house." Einstein also said, "If I were given one hour to save the planet, I would spend fifty-nine minutes defining the problem and one minute resolving it."

While that may sound extreme, it does highlight the importance of defining problems. It also hints at an interesting corollary. A well-defined problem often contains its own solution within, and that solution is usually quite obvious and straightforward. By defining problems properly, you make them easier to solve, which means saving time, money, and resources.

Problem solving is at the heart of all inventions, of social and cultural evolution, and is the basis for market-based economies. The ability to find solutions is essential.

Many times in my career I have attended project meetings, brainstorming sessions, and meetings in general, all designed to tackle one problem or another. Usually, there was no real outcome. Not only were these meetings a waste of people's time, they were lost opportunities. The problems that were supposed to be addressed in those meetings were real and important; the fact that no solutions for them were found meant that problems persisted — and the companies suffered. To avoid this, companies need a new approach to problem solving. They need to change how they handle fixing broken programs and initiatives. They need a structured approach, one that is creative, agile, open-minded, and reflective, while bringing in diverse thinking to drive innovation.

Problem solving is outcome-based. You need to get to an outcome — something needs to happen to drive things forward. You know that there has to be an end. Many times, companies get caught up in busy work, which is not outcome focused. My method will help drive results.

You need to analyze a situation. You need to think critically about the situation and reflect. You need to look at things from different lenses and perspectives, and dissect them. Critical thinking is integral to the problem-solving approach. It involves logically analyzing data and events.

Critical thinking is self-directed, self-disciplined, self-monitored, and self-corrective. It presupposes assent to rigorous standards of excellence and mindful command of their use. It also requires a commitment to overcome our native egocentrism and sociocentrism. It is necessary to identify and exclude extraneous influences that might prejudice your analysis, such as egocentrism and bias.

We are all prone to egocentrism and bias. The key is to recognize it and to work at excluding their influence in the identification of problems and our proposed solutions for them.

In her article "A Linguistic Perspective on Egocentrism," Thora Tenbrink writes:

> We do not naturally appreciate the point of view of others or the limitations in our own point of view. We become explicitly aware of our egocentric thinking only if trained to do so. We do not naturally recognize our egocentric assumptions, the egocentric way we use information, the egocentric way we interpret data, the source of our egocentric concepts and ideas, the implications of our egocentric thought. We do not naturally recognize our self-serving perspective.

To be a successful problem solver, you need to ignore your own ego. In fact, the very act of problem solving involves thinking about something else. When you focus on an outside goal, you are forced to look beyond yourself.

Just as successful problem solving involves looking beyond bias and ego, it also necessitates examining the ideas of others. This requires you to respect others. You must look beyond your own biases — conscious or unconscious — and embrace diversity. In the end, of course, to successfully achieve a goal it is necessary to execute one idea, but the process of selecting the idea to act on should involve a careful examination of every idea, whatever the source. To be a successful problem solver you must be open-minded.

When a problem arises, companies very often hold meetings and invite everyone in order to solve the problem. Such meetings frequently end in failure because no real thought has been given beforehand to the exact nature of the problem and who might be best to solve it. My model provides a clear path, showing how to address some of these challenges. It creates a standardized approach, while bringing in diverse perspectives to solve problems.

## THE MODEL

There are four main phases to problem solving: problem identification, ideation, execution, and reflection. To lend clarity to the issues that need to be focused on, I have broken each of the phases down into a few steps to follow. In turn, I have broken these down further, converting the issues that need addressing to a series of questions that need to be answered. These questions are meant to provide you with a good understanding of what each problem solving phase is designed to achieve. The model has been designed to streamline thinking by bringing in diverse perspectives. This approach ensures that the teams in your company using this model are focused in their thinking.

The foundation for this model is innovation. Innovation should not be an afterthought; it should be at the core of how we think about the work that we do. For a company to succeed, everything it is, everything it does, everything it produces must be constantly reviewed and updated. Companies need to foster and support the creativity of their employees so they can tackle the new challenges that are constantly arising. They need to be more intrapreneurial. This model will show you how you and your company can do this.

The model provides a blueprint, showing how you can draw on the talents and ideas of your staff to generate the new ideas necessary to tackle the big problems your company is facing. And it will show you how to do so efficiently.

The model focuses on the lifecycle of an idea. It follows an idea from incubation to execution, explaining the problem solving techniques that will help you to overcome the challenges that will inevitably arise.

# COMMITMENT

## PROBLEM IDENTIFICATION

**STEP 1** — IDENTIFY PROBLEMS TO SOLVE OR PROJECT BASED ON CRITERIA

executive sponsor — 2 hours

**STEP 2** — IDENTIFY TEAM

executive sponsor — 1 hour

### GUIDING QUESTIONS
- What is the problem that you are trying to solve?
- What kind of problem is this?
- Have you seen a similar problem before?
- What information do we have or need to find?
- What kinds of people/teams do we need to solve the problem?
- What expertise or knowledge do we need in order to solve the problem?

## IDEATION

**STEP 3** — PLANNING TASKS AND ITEMS TO BE COMPLETED

team — 2.5 hours

### GUIDING QUESTIONS
- Do you have any initial ideas on how you might solve the problem?
- Have you solved similar problems in the past? What worked or what could you have done better?
- Who are your stakeholders?
- Are there any market trends or data that may impact the problem?
- What are the changes in customer behaviour or market conditions that may impact the problem statement?
- Which ideas would help me address the problem AND anticipate changes in the industry, market, or customer behaviour?
- Which ideas could I combine to achieve the goals?
- Does the idea make sense?
- Is the idea simple and easy to implement?

## IMPLEMENTATION

**STEP 4** — IMPLEMENT/TEST

### GUIDING QUESTIONS
- What is the change that you are going to make?
- What areas of the business do you need (e.g., HR, operations, marketing, engineering) in order to implement the change?
- How will it impact the various groups, teams, and customers?
- What is the new design or process you are proposing?
- How will you communicate the change?
- What is the timeline to implement the change?

## REFLECTION

**STEP 5** — REGROUP/REFLECT

### GUIDING QUESTIONS
- Have you solved the problem?
- Can you look back and see a simpler way to solve this problem?
- Can you succinctly summarize the approach you used to solve this problem?
- Was the process easy to apply?
- Have you incorporated bends in the road — sustainable problem solving?
- What could you have done differently?
- Is your customer happy?

## PHASE ONE: PROBLEM IDENTIFICATION

Success in business demands an ability to solve problems. If things aren't going right, you need to know what's wrong. You need to be able to look beyond the superficial and the obvious to discover the root causes of the problem. In short, if you don't know what the problem is, how can you solve it?

Problem identification is the first phase in my model. Identify the problem that needs to be solved, and then determine which team members can help solve the problem. These two steps go hand in hand. As you think about the problem, you will start to see which parts of the company need to be involved.

Most companies are organized by department. Projects have to pass through different departments in order to reach completion. This process is usually far too time-consuming and often involves too many people. It is inefficient. Bureaucratic inertia inhibits the completion of projects and, by extension, the success of the company. By replacing this structure with an intrapreneurial one, companies will become more nimble, which increases performance. Instead of relying on existing departments to process a problem, companies should develop project teams to quickly develop and execute solutions to problems.

To authorize this change and to champion specific projects an executive sponsor is needed. It has been my experience that having such a person is essential. If you don't have executive support, projects lose focus and attention. Priorities change in companies, so, in order to ensure completion, you need a senior leader behind a project. This person will act as the enabler should roadblocks arise and as the voice communicating back to the company if and when things go sideways. This sponsor will also ensure things keep moving along and are being executed.

Once you have an executive sponsor in place, you need to develop a team. The key here is to bring the right people to the problem. At this point, there is often a temptation to develop a large team so that you can benefit from people with a wide range of knowledge and differing viewpoints. You should avoid doing this. Limit the number of people around the table.

Gathering a massive squad for your meeting will only stifle creativity. As Rachel Gillett writes on fastcompany.com, "The idea of working within small teams is believed to help diminish various innovation killers like groupthink and social loafing."

For instance, project "kickoff" meetings often resemble company-wide free-for-alls where everybody and their friends are invited to attend. Employees take it upon themselves to forward invitations to others. Others feel they "need" to be there to feel included. We all want to be part of what is gong on, right? Well, there is being engaged and there is chaos. Put it this way: where do you feel more engaged at a concert: sitting in the front row or all the way at the back and high up in the nosebleeds? The more, the merrier may be good advice for having fun, but it doesn't make sense when it comes to launching a project.

I recall several times when thirty people or more were piled into a boardroom for a meeting. It was chaos. Too many people around the table induces groupthink — decisions are made as a group in a way that discourages creativity or individual responsibility. As a result, the project starts off on shaky ground.

Creating a successful project team involves identifying who should be around the table, which involves knowing why they should be there. My rule of thumb is that the core team for any project should be made up of no more than four or five people. These are the people who will lead and represent their respective areas as they relate to the project. Each project team member has a specific role and responsibility. For a project, there should be a lead, a coach, and three key team players.

How do you go about identifying the people for your project team? This depends on the nature of the problem that needs to be solved. Once that has been determined, you'll be able to find the people you need to solve that problem.

Here are a few questions that will help you to manage this process.

## What Is the Problem That You Are Trying to Solve?

Although it is a generic question, it is really important because it makes clear to the team that there is a need that must be met. What is it? The people on your team are likely to answer that question differently. This is a good thing because you will capture different perspectives and you will see the problem from different angles.

## What Kind of Problem Is This?

This question will force the team to dig deeper. Is this a product design problem? Is it a customer experience problem? Is it a marketing, HR, or operations problem? Digging deeper helps you to get closer to the fundamentals of the problem.

## Have You Seen This Kind of Problem Before?

This is really important because sometimes within companies similar problems have arisen before. Are there patterns, ideas, or themes that you have seen previously? If this is the case, you can see what was done in the past, learn from the example of those who tackled them, determine what mistakes (if any) they made, and then decide how you may need to modify their approach to handle the situation you are facing. This exercise of going back or thinking about reoccurrences and similarities helps one to come closer to the root problem.

## What Information Do You Have or Need to Find?

I go back to my chapter on first principles ... getting to the facts, and not basing things on assumptions. What are the facts, truths, and pieces of data that you currently know and what are the other types of information that you need to gather in order to get closer to formulating the problem? This is all about getting to the root of the problem, and laying the foundation.

## What Kinds of People Do You Need in Order to Solve the Problem?

With a clear understanding of the problem you are trying to solve, it's time to put together the best team for the job. The people you select for your team, with their special talents and areas of knowledge, will bring the project to fruition. Their special combination of chemistry, capabilities, and skill will create great output.

There are five specific types of people you should be looking for to create the greenhouse effect within your company. Each one is a type of intrapreneur, and their traits and personalities are key for innovation, growth, and solving problems. These people adopt specific roles in executing ideas. If you look within your company at the people who already work for you, you may recognize these five types of people among them.

- **Disruptors.** These are the curious among your people. They ask lots of questions, push the boundaries, and probe business models and why things are done the way they are. They are the people who make you think, who make you see things in a different light. They look at what is coming next and propose ideas on how to be better with potentially new business ideas and methods. These people are particularly disruptive because they are asking people to change, and we know that people are very uncomfortable with change.

- **Researchers.** Your researchers are the people on your team who are always reading and learning. Leverage their thirst for knowledge. These are the people who are on the hunt for information and ideas, always looking intensely at what is going on in the world outside. They need little direction because they will always find answers. If you need information on anything, these people are highly resourceful and will find you answers.

- **Trendspotters.** These are the people in your company who always know what is coming next. They are culture and lifestyle enthusiasts. They travel in the pursuit of knowing how the world lives and how we can all learn from other cultures. They are constantly observing and have a strong sense of where things are going and what the next big idea or trend could be.

- **Mavericks and rebels.** These are the people who take risks, who colour outside the lines. They are comfortable with taking a risk and failing. They can recover quickly and pick up the pieces and keep going. They are comfortable with bending rigid rules; they know how to navigate them in order to achieve high results. These are the non-conformists, the ones who are not afraid to disagree and challenge norms. These people are not afraid to speak their minds.

- **Connectors.** Your connectors know what linkages are necessary to ensure that your project is fully executed. They are able to see which areas need to be involved in order to make projects happen. They know the people within each area and they can connect them in order to achieve set goals. They know the right people and want to help when they can. They have a vision and knack for bringing pieces of a puzzle together. They make suggestions on how to enhance an idea through further discussions with like-minded people.

Now, you won't always have the luxury of picking and choosing as easily as this; people are not robots. We can't be programmed on command. But generally a good team should be comprised of individuals roughly consistent with the five types described above. Empower them to do their best work together. And at the beginning, you especially need to allow them to make a healthy share of mistakes. Your job as a team leader or department head is to make sure the mistakes are fixable. Don't put them in charge of the red button, in other words. Monitor, but motivate. When you can have these people work in the right way together ... the result is magical.

Once you have answered all of these questions, you should now be able to identify the problem. The next phase is ideation. At this point, you will draw on the creativity of your team to come up with possible solutions to the problem you are tackling.

## PHASE TWO: IDEATION

I've mentioned already that I believe everyone has creative capabilities, but that we have forgotten how to use them.

This process is designed to bring out ideas in people, to make them think about things differently, and reframe the problem as they need to.

Do You Have Any Initial Ideas on How You Might Solve the Problem?

When presented with a problem and asked to propose a solution to that problem, most people will come up with something. Usually, this is based on what they have read, what they have done, what they have thought — something from their past. All of this is valuable. Your team's ideas, knowledge, and experience should be collected and reviewed. When looking toward the future, it's important to have a clear view of the past.

### Have You Solved Similar Problems in the Past? What Worked, What Could You Have Done Better?

The point here is to think about similar problems that your team, your company, or the market has seen in the past? Review what worked in the past, then decide what you can take, what you should drop, and what you can adapt.

### Who Are Your Stakeholders?

This is perhaps the most important question that you need to ask yourself. If you don't know who your stakeholders are, it's impossible to craft a solution that will satisfy their needs. Identifying them is essential. Problems don't exist in a vacuum; considering context is fundamental to finding a solution to a problem. Only when you know who your stakeholders are and what they need can you find a solution.

### Are There Any Market Trends That May Impact the Solution?

This question, too, involves context. When considering the possible solutions to a problem, it is important to look not just at the needs of a department or a team. You must also consider the competition, new technologies, and changing government rules and regulations.

### What Are the Changes in Customer Behaviour or Market Conditions That May Impact the Problem Statement?

You must consider the needs of your customers. To remain relevant, your company must always be looking outside itself. You need to anticipate changes in the market and devise plans that take all of these things into account.

This is a deliberate activity and it involves answering these questions:

- What is influencing changes or changing behaviour in your customers?
- Has the context in which your customer exists or operates changed?
- What is the customer experience? Have customer expectations changed?
- How are customers interacting with your company, products, and services?

- How have your customers' needs evolved?
- How can you take all of this information and incorporate it into your thinking and ideation?
- Which ideas would help you address the problem and anticipate changes in the industry?

The answers you come up with need to inform the ideas your team comes up with for a solution to the problem. There should be a direct correlation. When you create linkages, then you are performing meaningful work. Finding the answers to these questions will allow you to get to the root of the problem your team is tasked with solving. These answers provide the guiding principles you must follow to achieve a successful outcome for the project. You're solving a problem rather than just doing work for the sake of work.

### How Do Project Teams Develop Outcome-Oriented Ideas?

There is a simple answer to this question: collaboration.

Collaboration involves working together with someone to produce or create something. That seems like a simple enough idea. However, true collaboration occurs far too infrequently in companies. Why? Because it is confused with "inclusivity" — the idea that people and their ideas must all be taken into account when designing or executing a project. When a project is being designed or executed, the North Star should always be the goal of that project. What tends to happen, though, is that along the way office politics intrude and people become worried that they will offend others. And so, to avoid upsetting the status quo, to ensure that everyone is included, people make decisions that serve those goals, not the goals of the project.

The reality is, to create ideas that will result in meeting the goal of a project, it is necessary to select, refine, iterate, and deselect ideas with the project's interests at heart, absent of ego and bias. A team that is truly collaborative will work to that end.

The only thing of importance is discovering what ideas work to achieve the project's stated goal. Keeping this in mind will force team members to think about which ideas will result in achieving the desired state and to focus on the output of the project.

### Does the Idea Make Sense?

This is a deceptively simple question that turns out to be much harder to answer than is immediately apparent. The first question is, who does it make sense for? It seems obvious that ideas that make sense to everyone inside the company may not make sense to those outside the company. As I stated earlier, the best idea is of little use if it can't be executed. We must think about the realities of implementation. How complex is the idea and how feasible is it to implement?

It takes a great deal of talent to push creative boundaries while also managing to execute those creative ideas in the real world. If you want to push creative boundaries, rather than be bounded by process, governance, etc., you need to be able to identify the limiting rules that cannot be avoided, and at the same time explore those accepted rules that can, in fact, be bent or broken.

### Is the Idea Simple and Easy to Implement?

This question plays off of the previous one. As we know, ideas are just ideas until they are executed. Most people become discouraged and unmotivated when thinking about implementation. Just imagining the number of sets of approvals, steps, and layers that are necessary to navigate to make things happen is overwhelming. It doesn't have to be.

Rather than looking at the overall process, it is often helpful to consider the various steps involved in executing an idea. What are the actual things that need to happen in order to achieve what you need to achieve? Is the task really difficult or can we break it down to its basic form and achieve what we need to?

Remember the story about Elon Musk and the electric car battery? The idea of that may have been explored in the past, but it was not pursued because people thought it was too expensive ... then someone else came along and explored it, and, well, did it.

## PHASE THREE: EXECUTION

Successfully executing an idea is difficult. That needs to be said. The real test of a project team is finding a way to execute the ideas that they have been tasked to create to solve the problem. Not only must a workable plan be designed, that plan must be carried out successfully so that the team's goal is reached. This requires ingenuity and determination.

In each phase of the problem-solving process, there is a danger that some or all of a project team will lose sight of something: the problem to be solved; the ideas under consideration; the idea that is to be executed; the execution plan; the goal. Maintaining clarity is essential for the success of the project. There can be no miscommunication.

A perfect example of how miscommunication can arise is the game "broken telephone." People sit in a circle, and one person whispers something into their neighbour's ear. That person then whispers what they heard into the next person's ear and so on, until the message gets back to the original person. The more people involved, the more scrambled the message is likely to be at the end of the chain. The lesson of the game is that basic communication gets lost when you have too many people involved.

The number of people involved in transmitting a message is not the only source of confusion, however; people not only mishear messages, the fact is that human beings also tend to hear what they want to hear. Messages and information get lost, misrepresented, re-imagined, or completely misconstrued as word travels.

The typhoon-like surge of information that characterizes the modern business environment can overwhelm even the most organized and imperturbable of employees. In addition, inefficiently organized work environments, shifting company priorities, and ineffective project management habits and practices can — and do — undermine an employee's efforts to achieve their goals. If this is true of a company, taken as a whole, it is little wonder that project teams also suffer from the same problem.

Of course, no matter how talented a project team is, it needs the resources, skills, and knowledge of many parts of the company to ensure the success of its project. Failure to get buy-in from the rest of the company leads to failure of the execution process.

The way to avoid this, as I have said before, is to remind everyone that they must all be in the business of solving problems. We are all problem solvers regardless of what industry we are in, what department we are in, what our job is. We simply use different skills as a means to solve them. Whether you are in marketing, HR, finance, or operations, you are on a mission to solve problems and generate solutions. What makes my model unique is that it takes this process a step farther, so that the problems in each critical phase on the path to execution are actually assigned, to ensure the work gets completed.

* * *

It's time to execute.

This is the point where you take the ideas, crystalize them, and put them into action. Here are the questions that you need to ask yourself in order to successfully execute your project team's plan.

## What Is the Change That You Are Going to Make?

Now that you have gone through the ideation part of the problem-solving process, you need to be completely certain of the idea that you are planning to execute. This is the phase where you are forced to make a decision about the best path forward. The art of articulation is key. You start to visualize and realize what you must do going forward.

## What Areas of the Business Do You Need in Order to Implement the Solution?

To execute an idea, you need to identify the people, departments, and functions that will be needed. Then you must take things one step farther: you need to imagine all the potential roadblocks that might arise and threaten the project's goal, and then you have to identify the people you may need should such roadblocks appear.

## How Will the Achievement of the Project Team's Goal Impact Other Groups and Teams? And, Most Importantly, How Will It Affect Customers?

When change happens or you are trying to implement change, the most challenging job is finding a way to bring people along on the journey. You must be able to explain why change is happening, why it is needed. Of course, before you can explain those things to people, you need to have asked those questions of yourself — and you need to have found acceptable answers.

The "why" dictates what you plan to do and how you plan to do it — that is, how you plan to accomplish the changes that you say are necessary. In order to explain those, it's best to have facts to back you up. I have always led with data and facts when presenting problem-solving plans, because it's possible to use data and facts to argue in a compelling and engaging way. When you present compelling arguments, people very naturally want to be a part of what you're doing.

## What Is the New Design, Process, or Program That You Are Proposing?

Answering this question will force you to further refine your solution. If you cannot clearly articulate what it is that you are proposing, then it will not be implemented successfully.

## How Will You Communicate the Change?

While most large companies have communications departments, and even small companies will employ communications specialists on a contract basis, the value of communications, both within companies and as a sales and marketing tool, is often unrecognized. The fact of the matter is, communication is what connects people.

Remember that at every phase, effective communication is absolutely essential. Problem identification, ideation, execution, and reflection — all depend on clear communication among team members, and between them and project managers, and across and up the different rungs of your company's structural hierarchy. Ideally, the hierarchy is organized to maximize the flow of communication. Too many uncrossable moats and walls that are too high are communication roadblocks that will undermine performance and lead directly to mistakes that threaten quality. To ensure the success of your project, you must articulate what message needs to be delivered to whom and when. A well-thought-out communications strategy is vital.

## What Is the Timeline to Implement the Change?

Many times we leave meetings with no timelines for the action items discussed. Asking this question and getting an answer will give you the information necessary to ensure that your team is able to look at the project from a feasibility perspective. They will be able to say to themselves: Let's look and see what we need to do to make it happen. Let's see when we need to get that done by. Let's take the idea and put it into action.

## PHASE FOUR: REFLECTION

American philosopher, psychologist, and education reformer John Dewey said, "We do not learn from experience ... we learn from reflecting on experience." This is very true. However, the benefits of reflection are not recognized in many companies. In almost every company where I have worked, projects were conducted in a fast and furious manner. There was no time allowed for reflection after completion of a project.

In one of the first companies I worked for, however, I was taught the discipline of reflection. I was instructed on how to do a post-project review, and a win/loss review (in cases of sales). There is much power in doing this. Reflection requires discipline, but it yields so many benefits.

After the high of creating amazing work, you need to be able to savour what you've accomplished, and think about it. There is such power in thinking. What did you like about the work you did ... that the team did? What should you have done differently? What have you learned? What can you take away to make you stronger ... to make you better?

Reflection helps to make projects stronger, it provides extra knowledge to the company so that change can be handled more effectively in the future, and it provides you and your team with knowledge. There are many things that can be taken away from a period of reflection following the completion of a project. There is one vital question that must be asked during this period.

### Was the Problem Solved?

It is a simple yet powerful question. Being able to honestly see if you were able to achieve what you set out to do is crucial. Your success, your team's success, the company's success all depend on solving problems. So, just as it's crucial to be able to identify problems in order to help a company succeed, it's also crucial to be able to determine if the plan taken to solve a problem actually worked. You need to ask yourself: Can I look back and find a simpler way to solve this problem? Can I succinctly summarize the approach that I used to solve this problem? Was the process easy to apply? Have I incorporated bends in the road? Is the solution a sustainable one? What could I have done differently? Is the customer happy?

Now you have the blueprint, a standardized method to deal with the problems and challenges within a company. The four main phases — problem identification, ideation, execution, and reflection — keep your team focused on their thinking so they can create innovative ideas to solve the problems facing your company. Next we'll use this model to solve a typical problem.

# CHAPTER FIFTEEN

## Applied Learning

NOW THAT YOU HAVE SEEN the model, let's apply the methodology to a real life case study, starting at the very beginning.

Imagine you are a marketing practitioner and are constantly dealing with problems on a day-to-day basis. Your focus is digital, where most of your customers live. They are on the internet, scouring news, obtaining information, making comparisons on how to make their purchases or how to decide on products and services that they want to buy.

Your company website is the destination point that most of your prospective customers go to for information. They go there to obtain information about your company, your products, and your services. You want to attract traffic, so one of your jobs is to gain information about the types of people visiting your website.

- What are the demographics?
- What are they looking for?
- How can you best engage with your customer base in order to create leads, but also develop a better understanding of these individuals?

These questions are, in essence, tools. Tools that will help you get closer to your customer.

Data analytics is an increasingly important element of website development. In this case study, imagine you've been tasked with capturing data sets from your website traffic to help you see trends and patterns that will enable you to do some kind of predictability work.

\* \* \*

Now let's get specific. Your marketing role is within a multipurpose technology company offering several different products and services to a wide array of customers. Your site offers many different demos and trials, all designed to capture information about your online visitors. There is a problem, though, with a particular product suite that your company is interested in selling. The potential customers that the company site is attracting seem to be ignoring the free trial being offered for that suite and you are losing them during their visit.

This information has come to light through your web analytics. Visitors' duration on the site is brief, and their journey through the site has been disjointed. Visitors aren't signing up for the free trial and they also aren't opting in for more information, so you aren't getting any details about them or their businesses.

You've read some of the criticism: it isn't "user friendly"; it's cumbersome; it's kind of boring; "I don't get it." Visitors to the site have commented that the demo you're offering takes too long to activate. There are several forms and boxes that customers need to click prior to launching the demo, but few bother to click on them all. It seems that there are so many that most potential customers lose interest in the demo.

This is very valuable data. The actions — or the lack of action — taken by potential customers can be appropriated by you and used for intelligence when you are planning your work.

## STEP ONE: PROBLEM STATEMENT

Based on the above information, let's start to think about what kind of problem this could be.

Is it a web optimization problem? Web optimization refers to more than just search engine optimization. It can also include things like improved performance on the site to drive the right outcomes.

In this particular instance, what is the desired outcome? Is it to have the website visitor click through demos to experience the product, or is it to have them download a free trial?

When I spoke about framing and reframing the question, this is an example of why the problem statement is so important. You can slice and dice this problem in many ways, but if you don't have clarity on what the problem is and what outcome you want, then going through a process of trying to solve it will be futile.

It is really important to dive deeper into the problem statement/question.

Based on the data analytics that show site visitor usage patterns, it is clear that the site is not capturing the right kinds of information at the right time with the right kind of customers. So, how do you ensure that you are attracting the kinds of customers you want? And then how do you take those customers and harvest them into leads and, ultimately, loyal customers?

These questions lead us to another set of questions. How do we maximize leads in the customer journey by creating a compelling experience online? How do we capture quality data in order to better serve and understand our customers through value-added content? And because this is a multipurpose technology company, the success (or lack of it) of the other product groups offered on the company website may offer useful insight for solving the problem related to the particular suite under consideration. Are they seeing high drop-off rates also? What are their journey maps like? How have they determined patterns of their customer base and how are they making use of it?

Tapping into the knowledge and experience of other parts of the company can yield vital information. This kind of cross-departmental learning is crucially important, and, as I said earlier, we have much to learn from each other and the approaches that we take. Being able to leverage information to company or product advantage can help you better understand the context of your problem and prepare you to think about it in the right ways.

## STEP TWO: PROJECT TEAM

Once the problem has been identified, it's time to put together the team.

Does size matter? Okay, settle down, guys. Look, when it comes to putting together an excellent team, quality really is the only criteria. So, yes, size does matter, but only in terms of it being the *right size* for the job. Companies often make the mistake of assuming that if two people can do a job, then four can do the same job in half the time. Faster, right? Simple! Well, not necessarily. Problem solving is less linear than exponential. Two team members can do ten times more than a team twice its size . . . if you find *the right* two team members.

Steve Forbes told me a favourite business anecdote of his came from Amazon's Jeff Bezos. He calls it "the pizza rule." It is pretty simple. Never invite so many people to a meeting that two pizzas cannot feed the entire group. Companies are famous for having more people than required — a result of trying to be diplomatic and inclusive. This is a mistake.

In the list below, you'll see the layout of what the team should be.

- **One executive sponsor.** The role of the executive sponsor is to be the champion for the project, the person who will help the team remain focused. In a corporate environment of shifting priorities and a fight for resources, the team sponsor will ensure that the resources of the company necessary for the project will be maintained until the project is completed, and that people will not be shuffled around.

  This is also the person who will help with removing roadblocks. This person will act as the enabler, helping the project team to navigate the processes and approvals set up by the company to ensure that the work moves through the systems when required.

- **One project lead.** The project lead is the project manager for the team. I wrote earlier about the need for good project management. Organization and direction ensure clear accountability of the project. The project lead is accountable for establishing deliverables, tasks, milestones, dates, assigning work to people within the team, and tracking progress and outcomes. They are also responsible for identifying any potential risks, should they arise, and communicating that, if necessary, to the executive sponsor for support.

- **One coach and facilitator.** The coach and facilitator is designed to take the team through the process. They ensure that all elements of the process are met and push back to dig deeper if the team needs to. They are responsible for ensuring that the team stays on track, that they do not diverge from the process or get sidetracked.

- **Project team.** The project team should consist of three to five people. While we want the disruptors, mavericks, and researchers, we know that we need cross-functional people on this team in order to solve problems. So let's go back to the problem at hand.

We know that this is a digital marketing lead-generation problem. What job functions make the most sense to have around the table? Because this is a web problem, it makes sense to have a person from web design and data analysis. Because the content may be in question — what is on the site and how customers are using it — it would make sense to have a content person. What about adding a creative thinker? The two identified are discipline experts, if you will, so let's add one person who may be able to add a fresh and unique perspective. Perhaps one of the profiles we talked about, a trendspotter or researcher?

This is a team of five working people. The idea is to keep the team lean and small so that work can get done. If they need to engage more people on their respective sides, then they can do so.

This is your team.

## STEP THREE: PLANNING AND IDEATION

It is now that most of the work, ideation, and planning will come together. Step three has five sub-steps. I'll present them as questions.

1. Does the team have any initial thoughts on how we might address the problem?
2. Have you seen this problem before?
3. Who are your stakeholders?
4. What are the trends in the market or data that you can use for this particular problem?
5. Which ideas would help you address the problem and anticipate the impact of any anticipated changes?

Step one involves the team's initial thoughts on how to address the problem.

Most of the time, it is unclear what exactly the problem is, but when you have a good problem statement, you start to very naturally see things more clearly. When we are clear on the problem, clear ideas and solutions start to appear.

The problem with the suite and the website is clear. There is only one option for the customer — to click on a demo — and it is clear that customers are not doing so. How can this be fixed? What if customers were offered more of a journey and they had some choices? What if there were two to three choices on something that was more interactive?

Let's move to the next big question. Have you seen this problem before? Has the problem existed within other team members' areas? When you looked to your peer groups, what worked for them? One thing to keep in mind here is that your peer groups have different audiences for different product categories. What might work for one group may not work for another. Audience is key; what is important to one group, another will prioritize differently.

Sometimes when we work in companies, we make assumptions that if one area of the business did something and it worked, it will work for us as well. Again, going back to first principles, we cannot assume such a thing.

Learning from the lessons of the past and the experience of others is good, but you need facts (truth) if you want to truly realize the benefit of past lessons and experiences. Too many times you see copycat behaviour based on assumptions. It seems as though it is an efficient way to operate, but you may have to go back and redo the work if you haven't done the research up front.

Who are your stakeholders? This is a significant sub-step in the ideation phase. Who will be the people visiting the site? Are they small business owners looking for tools? Or are they technology practitioners in a large company? These are very different kinds of people with different objectives. Let's say, for the purpose of this exercise, that the potential customers are small business owners. Once that is determined, it's time to summarize the needs of those people.

- Small business owners want to be hyperproductive and will rely on technology tools to help them get there.
- They want these tools to help them be better organized.

- They will need the tools to be set up in order for them to potentially scale their business.
- The tools should be easy to use.
- Small business owners do not have big budgets like large companies, so the product should be priced accordingly.
- Small business owners need to work from anywhere at any time, so having freedom via the cloud is also going to be very important.

Bottom line: You need to know your customers. Are there changes in customer behaviour or market conditions that could impact how you ideate a solution? Asking questions is the best and most reliable method for connecting as directly to your customer base as practicable. And it isn't enough to ask questions and become complacent with the answers. You need to keep asking questions. The process never ends, okay? There is never a point when any CEO can confidently proclaim, "I know my customer!" The best any business leader can do is work as hard as they can to *keep* knowing their customer.

Companies are as hidebound as individuals. They have their biases and prejudices, preferences, beliefs, and habits the same as we do. Companies suffer from insularity. In short, "they don't get out enough." They become too confident and complacent with the ethos — too satisfied with the opinions, ideas, experiences, attitudes and behaviours of people within the company that they assume it's a snapshot of what the world looks like "out there."

It isn't.

The consequence, of course, is that instead of appealing to the customer, the emphasis shifts to meeting or gratifying the needs and the priorities of management or other stakeholders. The solution to this problem is to look beyond the environment of the company, to scan the market, observe, track, learn. This process becomes easier the more you do it, and it provides huge benefits. You become plugged in to the market.

Our next question, then, looks outside of our company. What are the trends in the market or data that you can use to solve this particular problem? We know that usage of the demo is low and we have some stats about time on the site, so we can infer that the content is not compelling to the end user. Something is missing.

Let's think about it for a moment. What are some of the things that are happening? Well, customers, like everyone else, suffer from information overload. Customers are being bombarded with information. It's impossible to assimilate everything, and, in trying, their attention spans become shorter. Customers need bite-sized information that is easily digested.

What can you do with this knowledge? It's useful, but it's not enough. You'll need to do some research. It is important to pause and go find information that will help lead you to the right solutions.

In such situations, most people will take the easy route and look to competitors for information. It's good to know what your competitors are doing, of course, but I have always believed the "me too" approach is unimaginative. Go to your customer.

I think that it is also important to go to sources that inspire creativity. That is why, in the chapter on curiosity, I mentioned the value of observing and reading. You always get inspiration when you pay attention to the world outside your office, to what people are doing beyond work. If you observe others and allow your imagination some space, you can bring that inspiration into the office and use it to help solve the problem facing you.

Go see what's happening beyond the corporate world. By observing real people living their lives you'll be able to see what is coming next, the next wave. You can harness the innovation of the world beyond your company's walls and be the trailblazer.

From observing the world and the actions of people, we know that they respond better to visual content than they do to text, so video content is important. You need to make your content accessible to your customers as they move about, working and living their lives, so the content needs to be mobile friendly. Look at people on the street, in bars, sitting on the subway. Everyone is looking at their phones. We are glued to them.

Like everyone else, small business owners want content that is convenient to access and easy to understand. They are moving very quickly and don't have time to read.

So, we have a bit more knowledge, but we need to know more. How are your competitors presenting their content on the web? What do small business owners care about when consuming content and learning about tools that could enhance or advance their businesses? The answer to these questions will help you to discover why it is that your customers are not downloading the trial offer for the suite, why they are choosing not to access the information that you are providing about it. In other words, why do the visitors to your company's site feel that it's not worthwhile to look at what is being offered? You need to answer that question in order to change their behaviour, to get them to download the trial offer, which will allow you to collect information from them about their businesses.

Okay, let's keep going to the next sub-step. Which ideas would help you address the problem and gauge the impact of any anticipated changes? We already looked at initial ideas above. We know that the original trial or demo was too static and not interactive. Customers want interactivity, they want video, they want visuals, they want it to be short, they want it to be engaging, to educate, to inspire. People also want an element of self-service.

So, what if you could focus on creating a more engaging experience that provided a couple of options? A video maybe? Perhaps a how-to and/or a more immersive experience, where one could simulate their environment? Perhaps more of an example of how the technology could be used in their work? This would be a much more meaningful way to engage and would make the information relevant.

People will purchase products that are useful to them. They want something that fulfills their needs. So, your products need to do that. But you don't want to offer something that appeals to only a very small number of customers. You want your products to have wider appeal. Is the content shareable? If you are able to create content that is smart, witty, and engaging, chances are that your end users will want to share it with their colleagues.

You can make it easier for site visitors to see how your product could be used in their business if your website allows potential customers to customize the how-to-use scenario for your product. Create an extension of the video that allows potential customers to apply the tool to their particular work environment. This would ensure that you are able to counter the "so what" attitude of site visitors. Allowing potential customers to see exactly how your product would work in their business will impress them, and it will help your company to gain much-needed information about potential customers so that you can increase sales.

All of this is a good start. But what exactly should the new content look like, and how can you create it? When it comes to producing a how-to video for a technology product, it can get complicated very quickly, so you need to think about how to make it interesting.

You know time is extremely valuable — not only to you but to your customers. Keep the video brief. Don't be the guest who won't leave the party on time. Research shows that direct appeals are less successful than compelling storytelling. People want to be engaged. It really doesn't matter what the product is; we respond to the story.

## STEP FOUR: EXECUTION

At this point we know what work needs to be done. Now a project plan needs to be developed in order to identify tasks, deliverables, timelines, and accountability. You need to create the work packets for the content and web design teams. The project plan is the responsibility of the project manager to lead and develop. They will assign tasks, instructing the appropriate team members to look at different ways to create content that is engaging for your customer base.

At this point, it is essential that everyone on the team completely understands what the ultimate goal of the project is, what the intermediate goals are, and what the timelines for delivering are. Once all are clear, the work can begin.

The bulk of the work for this project will be done by the creative side. They need to find some way to make the training video interesting. They will likely have some initial ideas, so it would be good, as part of this process, to have them create a few trial videos to see what works and what doesn't. Have the creative group create a few "look and feel" demo reels and get feedback from the core team on how they would resonate with visitors to the company's site.

Creating video that works is a tough balancing act. Company websites are designed to generate sales by allowing customers to purchase goods and services or by allowing them to see what the company has to offer them — this latter sales tool is designed to create leads for the company. In many cases, companies focus too closely on closing sales quickly. As a result, the content of their sites is unappealing — there is nothing on offer except the bare bones of the business. Selling should be the by-product of good content. To be successful, a company website really should be geared toward educating and inspiring.

Let's face it, people don't want to be sold to. People like being entertained and even feeling appreciated. If they can learn something, too, it's a plus. If your web content can satisfy your customers' desires, the company website will attract more people and they will stay on it longer. This will go a long way to meeting the goal of the project team.

One of the project team's goals was to capture customer data and learn more about the company's customers. Entertaining and informative web content that offers some tangible and immediate benefit to visitors will encourage potential customers to provide more information. This point needs to be foremost in the mind of the content specialist when they are building the solution.

In order to track progress, I would recommend a weekly check-in to see how things are going. Among other things, the role of the project manager is to flag any problems in the timeline and completion efforts.

Once your customers have voiced feedback on the original experience, you need to decide if it would be valuable to get their feedback on the new version of the video and training experience. A test or trial of the refreshed content would be good. This is an experiment that takes your customers' feedback into consideration. Before going live into production, you would want to build out a test before deployment. This feedback loop is critical in the development phase.

Designing the plan is very important, and I would recommend using a worksheet similar to the one I have provided for this example. This is a valuable tool for the project manager. As this work gets underway, it is important to stay close to the problem elements and to what the customer is looking for.

Don't forget to create a communications plan (a communication plan distills information amongst the company's stakeholders. It formerly defines who should be given specific information, when that information should be delivered, and what communication channels will be used to deliver the information, as well as the frequency of the information to be delivered). The changes to the website will impact a number of different parties, so you need to think about how to communicate the changes being made, and to whom, both internally and externally. Who in the company needs to know about this change and how will it impact them, if at all? Which communication vehicles will you use to do this? What will the message be, and how often do you need to communicate?

## IMPLEMENTATION
## WEB DESIGN AND CONTENT

| DELIVERABLE | OWNER | DUE DATE | STATUS |
|---|---|---|---|
| Self-serve video experience<br>• New video content | Jared Smith | March 25 | Complete |
| Live 1:1 Demo via phone<br>• Demo content | Jared Smith | March 11 | Complete |
| Re-design *Try now* page to *Getting Started* landing page<br>• Add 3 options buttons connected to new pages | Jennifer Baker | April 6 | Staging in progress — completed mid next week |
| Web layer — demo layer (1:1)<br>• Ensure Tele team is equipped to handle technical inquiries coming in | Charlie Parker | April 6 | Staging in progress — completed mid next week |
| Ensure Tele is aware of new self-serve video experience and can recommend to customers | Charlie Parker | April 6 | Staging in progress — completed mid next week |
| Staff a 1:1 phone demo with Partner for 2-day trial option | Charlie Parker | April 6 | In progress (March 28) |

Each element of the plan should be built out in work packets. The chart above is an example of the kind of progress check that can be used for a work packet.

This worksheet is for the portion of the overall plan relating to web design and content. Every other aspect of the overall plan should have its own work packet progress check chart. All aspects of a plan must be integrated to ensure that any changes made will be effectively communicated internally and externally. Creating work packets for tasks, and progress check charts for those packets will help to achieve this, easily and effectively.

The execution plan lays out the path that you need to follow to ensure that a project's goals are met on time. I wrote earlier about the importance of accountability for any project or initiative. Ultimately, it is up to the project manager to ensure that the project goals are met on time, and if something goes awry, they are responsible for seeing that appropriate action is taken by the team members (and others, if necessary) to get the project back on track.

To execute a project flawlessly, these questions need to be asked — and answered.

- **What is the critical path?** The critical path is the route that must be followed to get from the start of a project to its finish. This is the roadmap that will get you and your team to its destination — the successfully completed project. Not only should you and your team have a clear idea of this from the start, everyone should refer to it throughout the course of the project to ensure that you are still on the right path.

- **What are the milestones?** Every journey includes milestones, those important markers that indicate that progress is being made toward reaching the final destination. Your team's project will also have its milestones — accomplishments set out in the project plan that show that progress is being made and that the plan is on track. To ensure the project's success, it is crucial that the entire team knows what the milestones are and keeps them in mind.

- **What are the potential roadblocks that will hinder the success of the project?** Identifying the potential roadblocks that could interfere with the successful completion of the project will help to ensure success. The path to success will likely have a few hurdles on it; it's important that you are aware of them from the start and prepare yourself for dealing with them. These hurdles will test you and your team. To successfully complete a project, it's crucial that you and your team keep in mind the Boy Scouts' motto: be prepared.

## STEP FIVE: REFLECTION

When I was at TELUS, post-project reviews were held for each project. These were done no later than one week after the completion of the project. This gave the team enough time to think about the work that had been done and also to think about what could have been done differently. We would take those lessons and recommend how we might apply them to other projects moving forward.

Taking time to reflect will make you do better work. On a personal level, reflection enables you to develop self-awareness. When teams perform group reflection they develop better work awareness. What worked? What didn't? How might we tweak that process a bit next time? Yeah, that's a great idea! The point is, a heavily routinized and overly structured workflow creates zombies who sleepwalk through the process and disengage at every level possible. Team members who *routinely* have an opportunity to do new things *routinely* discover new and better and more creative — and ultimately more cost-effective — ways of doing things.

Ask yourself this: What is the difference between a groove and a rut? A rut is a routine that has become or grown stale. A groove is a routine that feels fresh and stimulating. So who is going to do better work? the employee in a groove or the employee in a rut?

The list below is designed to help you and your team find your groove.

- **Have you solved the problem?** Going back and thinking about the outcome is important. In the case of this scenario, the original problem statement was, "How do we maximize leads in the customer journey by creating a compelling experience for them? How do we capture quality data on our customers in order to better serve and understand them through value added content?" When you have completed the project, you and your team need to ask yourselves if you have actually accomplished the task that you set out to finish.

- **Was there a simpler way of approaching the problem?** One of the most important things to realize is that there is power in simplicity. People don't want unnecessary complexity, and anything convoluted will be hard to execute. Was the solution the team came up with the easiest and simplest that could have been devised? If not, are there further changes that need to be made?

- **Have you taken into consideration the sustainability of the changes that you have made? Is this solution going to get old too quickly?** When ideating, did you take into consideration developments in the future that may impact the long-term usefulness of your solution? Is the new feature that you developed able to be modified if future changes in the market necessitate it? It's important when designing new products and processes to build in flexibility so that these innovations can be updated when required.

\* \* \*

Do you see how you can apply this model in your work? Do you agree that clearly identifying a problem, obtaining the right insights, and going through the ideation and implementation phases in an organized way can help you reach new levels of problem solving and innovation? It is a very simple and pragmatic way to approach work.

This model fits the requirements for structure necessary for the successful running of any company, but it also allows intrapreneurs the opportunity to contribute. It demonstrates a way of using their creativity and talent to benefit all. In short, it provides a roadmap for how your company can use the talent and creativity of its employees in the most efficient manner to solve the problems that arise.

All of this, of course, will help you to better serve your customers. The most important question, after all is said and done, is, "Is the customer happy?" At the end of the day, this really should be the litmus test of whether you have achieved the goal. Making customers happy will make your company successful.

## BONUS EXAMPLE

Another real-life example of the importance of good leadership, and the consequence of its absence, can be seen in the fate of Toys "R" Us. Imagine how different the company's fate could have been. Toys "R" Us was an iconic and beloved brand for many people. It was the former leader in the toy industry; however, after years of slipping sales and mounting debt, the company had to file for bankruptcy.

This is a very familiar story; we have heard it many times. Every time it occurs, people ask, "Could bankruptcy have been prevented if management had acted differently? What if they had asked themselves the right questions and taken appropriate actions? What would the results have been?"

Let's use the model discussed above to see if we can discover what took place with this toy retailer. What was the problem? Because we are looking at the company from the outside, much of what we can say is speculation, but we can certainly try to assess the situation.

We know that sales were declining for years. Some may say that this was the problem, but this was an outcome of the problem. We have to dig deeper to better understand what was causing this. We need to find out more information. Consumers were not buying products. The question is, "Why?" What factors affect a customer's decision to purchase something?: the customer experience, how customers buy, their tastes and preferences, the products on offer, new entrants into the market that are enticing your customer base. All of these things will impact sales.

A greater understanding of what factors affect customer decision-making will uncover certain truths about what is going on. Once we determine and dissect that, the question becomes, does the current business model of Toys "R" Us need to evolve in order to accommodate all of the external changes and demands? Some of the external factors include competition from mass retailers, such as Walmart. These retailers offer a wide range of goods, from clothing to food to household goods, and they offer low prices. Such retailers have tapped into a trend in the market. People want to be able to buy multiple things in one destination because, with busy lives, they have a limited amount of time and don't want to have to go from store to store to shop.

- **Insight 1.** There is increased competition from other retailers, such as Walmart, who offer a wide variety of goods. People in today's nanosecond culture want to do more with less. These retailers have a solid online presence, as well, where many consumers do their purchasing. There is not a huge incentive to come into stores to purchase.

- **Insight 2.** Internet-only companies are another source of competition. Amazon and other businesses like it have become incredibly successful by offering customers a huge variety of goods at low prices. On top of variety of goods and low prices, the ease of browsing and the convenience of home delivery offered by these sites make them extremely appealing to modern consumers. Toys "R" Us did not really have a significant online presence and so it failed to capture a large part of that developing market.

- **Insight 3.** By design, Toys "R" Us stores are large and well stocked. As a result, they are difficult to navigate. Needless to say, this negatively impacts customers. Toys should be appealing, cute. Warehouse-like stores do not provide attractive spaces for appreciating the toys on sale. As a result, smaller, boutique-style toy stores have started to pop up. These stores showcase carefully curated items. The staff in these stores are usually more knowledgeable about the items for sale than are those in larger stores, such as Toys "R" Us. They are also likely to be more personable. The lesson is clear. Customers seeking items that satisfy an emotional need are drawn to smaller stores, ones that offer a more personal environment.

- **Insight 4.** The market has changed. Children are less drawn to traditional toys and the equipment needed to play sports. More and more, kids find their entertainment via computers and other electronic devices. There is less demand for the items on sale in a large-format store. To stay relevant, a company that focuses on the kids' entertainment market needs to take into account the change in the market.

How do we now take these insights and translate them into potential actionable items? These insights would require many parts of the company to participate and many would or could be capital intensive. In order to balance this, the exercise could be positioned as: Where do we invest and where do we divest? The point of this is not to undermine or oversimplify what went wrong with Toys "R" Us — it is much easier to see things when you are on the outside, and after things are all said and done — but to stress asking the right questions at the right time, then picking and choosing what you are going to do before it is too late.

The model is designed to do all this. Ask all the right questions when you are in the thick of it, when you are starting to see symptoms of the problem, before it becomes too big and too much of an undertaking to resolve.

# CHAPTER SIXTEEN

## From Silos to Tribes

THE KOROWAI LIVE deep in the jungle of Papua New Guinea. They lived without any knowledge of the outside world until they were discovered in 1974.

The Korowai live in clans of ten to twenty, with each clan made up of descendants of the same ancestors. These clans live independent of one another, relying on their family ties to survive. Isolated from the rest of the world, the Korowai depend on each other for their survival. In this type of environment, it is unlikely that families could survive if they operated in their own individual silos.

## SILO THINKING

Poor communication is probably the most common problem for most companies. Management keeps to itself, the upper-echelon executives rarely — if ever — step foot in the warehouse or coffee room, and employees complain about feeling isolated from the decision-making process and ignored.

In short, while we work *at* the same company, we aren't *in* the same company. We create and occupy silos. What goes on on one floor is never shared with what is going on on other floors. We keep to our silos. Ideas and experiences and intuitions — sources of innovation — that should be flowing gracefully up and down and across the company are blocked. It's like being forced to breathe stale, recirculated air, day after day.

This narrow mindset — silo thinking — doesn't make any sense. Projects and companies can only become stronger when people share information.

We need to remember and remind ourselves that we all share the same goal. We *are* the company — each and every one of us. Ultimately it is not *her* contribution or *his* contribution that matter but the sum total of *our* contributions. Silo thinking destroys the ideal of collective engagement. Instead of seeing the big picture, we focus on our own work, jealously guarding our domains, our projects, our tiny pieces of real estate as if that was the goal. Constructive collaboration is defeated by a silo mentality.

How does this happen? Typically, an individual, team, or department will elevate and prioritize its own agenda over the larger agenda — the true goal. They forget that their true North Star should be the success of the company, not a limited or short-term success (mine versus ours).

Nicholas Thompson is the editor-in-chief of *Wired* magazine and is a contributing editor at CBS and CNN International. He has spoken to some of the world's top leaders and thinkers. I spoke with him about the problems associated with consensus thinking.

He told me during our interview that rather than focusing on people problems, he focuses on his overall goal of creating an excellent magazine.

When there is a lack of shared focus on a common goal, he explained, when silos form and people no longer communicate and work together, imbalance, internal conflict, and competition arise. This not only leads to a poor work environment, it also hinders the success of the company.

Sometimes, silo thinking is not merely a symptom of a lack of perspective; sometimes it is an indication of a power struggle. Information is leveraged to enhance power. Rather than working together to help achieve success for the company as a whole, individuals, teams, or departments sometimes use their knowledge and work to benefit themselves, at the expense of others in the company and sometimes of the company itself. This is obviously a very dangerous situation; something that must be prevented at all costs.

Let's review the negative aspects of silo thinking.

- There are inefficiencies and redundancies between departments.
- Turf wars become a new reality with departments fighting over responsibility and ownership. Here we end up with a sandbox mentality.
- We see a lack of information sharing, where information becomes power, which results in power dynamics.
- There is internal competition for knowledge and resources.
- Different departments get valued more or less than others.
- We experience a general sense of unease and a lack of transparency.

It hardly matters at this juncture why your company is locked into silo-thinking. All that matters is that you act as rapidly as possible to deconstruct the silos and repair your company's culture. The stakes are far too high. Inattention, or placing the problem on the back burner and hoping it will go away or solve itself, is a prescription for certain defeat and a formula for obsolescence. The speed of globalization and its consequent effects — effects we have outlined in emphatic detail — are real. Silo thinking is not an option.

\* \* \*

Too much of what we do is what I call function dependent. Think of your business as a big checkerboard where each piece has a specific square to occupy. Finance has its finance square. Marketing has its marketing square. Public relations, accounting, research, and so on all have their squares. Only, in this game, a piece is never allowed to move. It has to stay where it is. Not a very fun game, is it?

If you are serious about breathing new life into your company structure, your focus must shift from function-dependant to goal-dependent thinking. When the focus shifts from the limited "here" to the larger "there," the goal — silos breaking down — will be reached.

Dismantling silos isn't easy. They have become a familiar and routine feature of the business culture. The list that follows will get you started.

- Why is the finance department just the finance department?
- Why is the human resources department just the human resources department?
- Why is the marketing department off by itself?

Functional-dependent departments breed silos. If you want true cross-team collaboration, you need to reorganize your departments, transforming them into goal-focused groups that integrate employees with the necessary skill sets.

Let's imagine that you work on the Apple sales team. You're getting all kinds of feedback on the design, functionality, and pricing of a new tablet. But because you work in the sales department, you're limited with regard to what you can do. After all, you're in the sales silo. What if, instead, you were part of a tablet team and you had access to a designer and an engineer to talk things through with? What if you, as a salesperson, could easily communicate the feedback that you've received from customers to the people who have the power to address concerns in the next iteration of the tablet? What could that do for overall product development and customer experience?

In my corporate experience, customers were encouraged to provide feedback. Great. I figured this kind of information was vital to the company in terms of delivering a better-quality product in the future. But too often there was no one in the pews who was willing to listen to the choir. If I tried to raise concerns or questions from customers, it fell on deaf ears. Colleagues around the table would nod and appear concerned, but a day or two later it was business as usual.

Meanwhile, customer complaints and concerns were piling up like old newspapers. At some point, of course, an executive or department head would come rushing into my office. "Why didn't I know about this?"

"Well, you did know. I told you and everyone else around that table about this problem months ago. In fact, I brought it up at several meetings in a row. I figured you knew."

Does that — or something like that — sound at all familiar? I thought so. We all do it. I call it the broken-record syndrome. I felt defeated. I felt depressed that I thought I could make a positive impact, but was being ignored. When we keep raising the same issue or providing insight again and again and no one is receptive, we eventually give up. (Unfortunately, that huge pile of customer complaints didn't go away!)

What happens when employees feel they have no power to make an impact on their company? What if they felt that they did have control? What if your teams had access to the people they needed to present feedback to who could contribute to positive corporate change?

The effect would be immediately positive. Such a change would start to motivate more of the right kinds of behaviour.

## TOWARD A TRIBE

The question is, can business teams organize themselves to produce outcomes that advance the goals of the company? The answer is yes — but only if certain requirements are met. Absolutely essential is a sense of unity. All members of the team must have a deep connection with one another and a shared vison of the goal that all are working toward. This is what binds them together.

Although all teams share the same ethos, each will have its own distinct makeup, one determined by the goal it has been tasked with achieving. That being said, the structure of all teams is the same:

- **Leadership:** Every team needs a leader. The leader makes decisions based on what is needed to achieve the goal of the team. In some instances, committees may be formed to help the leader in discharging their function.
- **Team membership:** The makeup of any given team is determined by the goal of the team. Some teams may include only members from the sales and marketing departments; others may include members from HR and management. In each case, the goal will determine who should serve on the team.
- **Common culture:** As mentioned, there must be a sense of unity in the team. A shared vision of the team's goal is essential, as is a common understanding of the beliefs and values that govern the way the company operates.
- **Egalitarian values:** The organization of the team should be egali-

tarian. There should be no institutionalized inequalities; hierarchy should not get in the way of good decision-making, and inequalities based on gender, ethnicity, etc., should not play a role. All should enjoy equal status and freedom.

Creating teams with this organizational structure and these values is both possible and necessary for success in business.

I am not saying companies should abandon, entirely, their traditional organizational structures; they need departments in order to foster the development of employees with unique and special skills. But what I am suggesting is that we re-imagine the way goals are pursued, the approach to problem solving. What is needed are multidisciplinary teams that share a common goal and a common culture. If we can change the traditional way of doing things to embrace this new way of thinking, we will have people coming together to work things out. Here's an example of a team based on these principles.

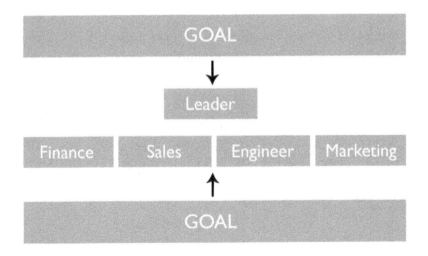

If we shift organizational structures from traditional departments to cross-functional teams, the result will be groups with diverse experiences and perspectives. The crosspollination that results from this will improve ideation. After all, how likely is it that a team made up of people who have the same expertise and who think the same way are going to be able to be truly innovative?

Creating cross-functional teams will help develop mutual understanding, an appreciation for other disciplines, and, going back to some of the original big ideas I opened this book with, it will address them as well.

- You would not be making assumptions about certain ideas or projects because you would have the people at the table to identify facts and truths.
- You would collectively, more openly, solve problems, and be much more productive and collaborative.
- You would be motivated by the right factors.
- You would have the right ratio of disruptors, mavericks, connectors, researchers, and trendspotters working toward a common goal.
- You would be focused on the output, having a set of values and a mindset that are in the best interest of the company.

You would not only survive the current and future industrial revolutions, but also become a force to be reckoned with.

# CHAPTER SEVENTEEN

## Nurturing Your Teams

**TO SATISFY THE NEEDS** and wants of your customers you need talented and dedicated employees. To remain successful and grow your company, you need intrapreneurs who will drive change by questioning the status quo, imagining better options, researching what is achievable, and exploring how goals can best be realized. Your job is to nurture the intrapreneurs in your company by ensuring that they have the resources and time to explore how your company can better serve its customers.

As an intrapreneur, I quickly came to realize that if I did not have the support of my manager, there was no way that I could accomplish the work I wanted to get done. The support of my managers gave me wings to fly. Sometimes, though, I did not have it, and in those cases my wings were clipped.

### DISRUPTION LEADS TO NURTURING

Accomplishing transformation in your company will make it necessary to disrupt the jobs of some people. It may involve replacing some people. Change does that. When you start to question things and challenge the status quo, you need to be prepared for disruption.

When transformation is taking place in your company, you need to support the people in your company who are completing the work. In my conversations with Raja Rajamannar, he indicated quite clearly that "management must walk the talk." What this means, essentially, is that if companies want innovation, executives need to truly support the behaviours that will drive this by

- supporting curiosity,
- encouraging debate, and
- supporting the people who question the majority.

Companies need to set up environments that are safe and comfortable for people to disagree. They need to take out fear, to empower people, and to stand behind them.

John Ruffolo, our innovation expert and CEO from OMERS Ventures, is suspicious when everyone agrees with him. "How could that possibly be," he asks himself, "when we are trying to break through?"

Employees need to be allowed to disagree. In fact, you, as a manager, need to cultivate open debate; you need to truly stand behind those who question the status quo, those who disagree. When you have your focused team members trailblazing through the company, there will be environmental noise, people who are happy with the way things are will oppose any new ideas and those who propose them. Leaders must support the intrapreneurs in the company by muting the noise so that the work can get done.

When I worked at TELUS, we had amazing leadership. My managers were focused on transforming TELUS, changing it from a telecommunications company to an integrated communications and technology company. Every project that I worked on was designed to achieve this goal. Teams were lean, creativity was encouraged, and as a result, change was accomplished quickly.

The process involved challenging norms, trying new things, pushing people to think differently; if we made mistakes, we learned together and moved on. While this work was difficult, it was extremely rewarding. I could move with fluidity and confidence because I had the active support of my leadership. I was happy and the work was a success.

I have also been in situations with poor leadership. The managers were unfocused, unclear; they were motivated by ego, and focused more on politics than on the work that needed to be accomplished. As a result, the team suffered and projects weren't successful.

My point is that people perform differently in different environments. This may seem obvious, but it is a truth that has enormous implications for the success of your business. If you don't supply the right kind of leadership to support your staff, they will not flourish. And neither will the company.

## SUPPORT AND REWARD

Having real intrapreneurial activity in your company is what will drive sustainable growth. The intrapreneurs need to be not only recognized, they need to be supported and rewarded. So, what should you be doing to support this kind of talent from within?

1.  **Recognize skills.** The first thing you need to do is recognize the skill sets of the people who work for you. I have discussed throughout the book the various types of intrapreneurs: the rebels, the researchers, the disruptors, the mavericks, the trendspotters. These are the people who are the thinkers, the ideas people, the ones who will challenge the status quo. But they are not doing it just for the sake of doing it. They are doing it to drive change, and to see new results because they are very outcome based.

2.  **Give creative freedom.** There is nothing more inspiring than to have your manager give you creative freedom to solve problems. When you have this, you take control, you take initiative, you take accountability. This is where magic really starts to happen. People start to ideate and think outside of conventional norms. Your role as the leader is to provide feedback and direction, but ultimately, you have to give your employees the chance to behave like true intrapreneurs when solving problems.

3.  **Provide access.** In order to make things happen, your people need resources. Providing your trailblazers with access to resources will allow them to realize their ideas. One of the most important resources the people on your teams need is time. As a leader, you can prioritize projects and this allows you to free up people's time to work on certain things. The role of the leader is to work alongside their peer groups to secure the time of different discipline groups, in order to give focus to such projects.

4.  **Make time.** I love learning. Curious people do. One of the things I've loved most in my career is learning — from those in different disciplines

and also from my managers. In a couple of my roles, my manager would, as part of our "catch ups," have a white board session. We would share ideas. He would teach me. All I wanted to do was to learn. But these sessions were mutually beneficial. I would communicate some of my challenges and we would learn from each other. This time was sacred to me and I needed it, we needed it. I needed it in order to be energized, refreshed, and, well, inspired. If you want to keep people engaged and interested, leaders must make the time to talk to their staff, good quality time.

5. **Be the advocate.** It is very easy to get sidetracked and displaced within a company. People will complain. The most important thing that you can do as a leader is to minimize the noise. When I was hired at Microsoft to help drive the transformation of the brand in the Canadian market, I had to make a lot of changes quickly. One of my manager's peers said to her, "Chitra is very disruptive." And her answer was, "I have hired her to be disruptive. That is her job." Creating change is difficult, and in order for the work to get done, leadership must back their people and support them through the journey. Communicate the what, the why, and the how your teams are doing, and support their work when they run into opposition.

6. **Reward behaviour.** If you want people to be disruptive, to challenge the status quo in order to drive change and help the company succeed, you must reward intrapreneurial behaviour. It is so easy to lose inspiration, to get caught up in corporate minutiae, so when your people are being brave, trying to pave new ways, you must recognize and celebrate these behaviours.

As a leader, you must acknowledge that people learn through observation. Through observation and familiarization, they will be more likely to engage in those same kinds of activities. It is critical that your behaviour — your approach to your job and how you relate to others — is consistent with what you say you want others to do.

The role of leadership, Steve Forbes told me, is to "marinate capable people." Everything depends on how you coach, support, and actively engage with your people as they transform your company, helping it to blossom and thrive. It's the spirit of the greenhouse approach.

# CHAPTER EIGHTEEN

## Final Thoughts

WE HAVE COVERED a lot of ground. We've drawn from big thinkers, taken lessons from some of the greatest minds of our time, from Darwin and Gandhi to Einstein and Galileo. We've looked at the brilliant ideas of Coco Chanel and Elon Musk.

We've read about groundbreaking thinking, visionary ideas, and have reflected on some of the greatest innovations from our past.

It has become clear that all of the world's greatest thought leaders have embodied qualities that forced people, businesses, companies, and societies to deviate from the norm for the greater good. I firmly believe that all of the world's greatest leaders have embodied elements of intrapreneurial thinking. They have challenged conventional thinking in their relentless pursuit of solving problems to drive meaningful change.

In the first part of this book, we looked at how we must rethink the rules, shifting away from accepted norms to new guiding principles that allow all employees, even the rebels and rogues, to do their best work. I shared my thoughts on consensus and majority rule. I noted how conflict is not negative — in fact, as we learned from visionary business leader John Ruffolo, dissent is what he looks for around the meeting room table.

We talked about the fact that humans must always be questioning things and asking why. We examined why you want curious people on your payroll — because curiosity is what drives innovation. And, of course, we also discussed the problem with basing decisions on assumptions, by digging more into the concept of first principles thinking.

Following this, we reviewed the seven principles that I believe companies must use to guide innovation:

- relevance
- creativity
- speed
- clarity
- accountability
- experimentation
- execution

Finally, I introduced my model: a simple, pragmatic way in which companies can solve problems, by bringing in elements of creative thinking, agility, speed, and all of the elements I've spoken about in this book. The model has presented you with a very simple way to apply methodology that will help drive the outcomes that you desire.

Now that we have reached the end of this book, we can all conclude that this is a universal truth — if you want to break through, in terms of innovation, you must deviate.

Somewhere along the way, humans and businesses seem to have lost that sense of adventure, falling into a state of complacency.

That complacency has driven companies to a place of struggle and contention. We saw that through the examples provided throughout this book.

We can all agree that innovation is something that every company, regardless of industry, struggles with.

I hope by reading *The Greenhouse Approach* you will agree not only that innovation is not the enemy, but also that innovation is not *that* difficult to achieve. What we need is new tools. When we have the right mindset, the right approaches, the right people, and the right disposition in place, the sky is the limit.

Remember, we humans tend to overcomplicate things. We come equipped with lots of baggage. The greenhouse approach is learning how to scale it back — to lighten the load — so that we don't have to work so hard at everything. Fact is, there are still only twenty-four hours to a day. The greenhouse is not about doing more, it's about doing it all better. The idea is to free up creative innovative-driven time by eliminating the time and resources wasted on routinized and counterproductive tasks.

Thinking back to Chapter Five, first principles thinking is not a new concept. The idea is that we have to get back to fundamental truths of ideas and ideologies. If you use this mindset, it will help you uncover things. The greenhouse approach model is about reflecting on the past and seeing what worked and what didn't, really uncovering fundamentals that will help drive you forward.

I think that companies have become confused. And in the words of Steve Forbes, "companies have lost their way." It's now all about going back to basics, going back to your core, back to what you know, and working from there.

We've tried to be everything to everyone, but sometimes the best innovations are those that are right in front of us. It's about finding different and unique ways of value creation. Remaining relevant with what's happening in the market and what's happening with your customers and your employees is what's going to help you stay ahead of the curve and maintain your sustainability.

## IF YOU TAKE NOTHING ELSE FROM THIS BOOK, LET IT BE THIS

Companies cannot rely on traditional organizational structures and traditional ways of doing business. They need to change in order to survive in the new world of work and in the new economy — full stop. Building a culture, a mindset, and an organization that fosters intrapreneurial thinking is the best way of doing so.

Innovation cannot be an afterthought. In order for companies to thrive, collective effort is needed. As we learned from the theories of adaptation and Darwinism, we must evolve. We want to build environments where people can come to do their best work. To do that, to channel the creativity and talents of your employees to problem solve and help your company succeed, you need to move beyond talk to creating a corporate culture that supports unconventional thinking. Let the creators — the rebels, the connectors, the trendspotters, the mavericks, the researchers — create. Give them the time and resources to imagine solutions to the problems your company needs to solve, and give them the resources and the accountability for accomplishing the programs they devise. My model identifies a very simple way of doing this.

In today's world, it can be very noisy. Information flows in from everywhere. Companies tend to waste time and company resources overanalyzing problems. They overcomplicate things. To solve problems, companies need to move away from this approach; they need to task small, creative teams to find the very basic questions that reveal the basic problems that need to be solved. Once that is done, the team — made up of intrapreneurs — can use their creativity to devise impactful innovations and meaningful solutions. Asking the right questions is the first step along the path that will lead to the desired goal.

Be curious, be open. Read, observe more. Listen. Reflect. Try something new. Be open to re-imagining conventional norms and ideas. Your actions will be illuminating.

# ACKNOWLEDGEMENTS

I WOULD LIKE TO thank all of the incredible sponsors and leaders in my career who have enabled me to be an intrapreneur; without their advocacy I would not have been able to accomplish the projects and initiatives that I undertook within their companies.

I am incredibly grateful to my thesis supervisors at Bradford University, who have guided and supported me through my doctoral research. With their wisdom and aid, my thinking evolved and I was able to refine ideas and concepts.

I am incredibly grateful to everyone who contributed to this book: John Ruffolo, Raja Rajamannar, Michele Romanow, Nicholas Thompson, and Steve Forbes. Their authenticity, openness, and gracious generosity in giving their time and thoughts have been incredibly insightful and impactful. Thank you.

I would like to thank my family for recognizing and supporting my pursuit of purpose driven work; this kind of work fills my soul.

Finally, deep gratitude to the team at Dundurn Press for believing in me and my work. Their support has been instrumental in helping me to complete this book.

# REFERENCES

Abatecola, Gianpaolo, Fiorenza Belussi, Dermot Breslin, and Igor Filatotchev. "Darwinism, Organizational Evolution and Survival: Key Challenges for Future Research." *Journal of Management & Governance* 20, No. 1 (2015): 1–17, doi.org/10.1007/s10997-015-9310-8.

Alpkan, Lutfihak, Cagri Bulut, Gurhan Gunday, Gunduz Ulusoy, and Kemal Kilic. "Organizational Support for Intrapreneurship and Its Interaction with Human Capital to Enhance Innovative Performance." *Management Decision* 48, No. 5 (2010): 732–55, doi.org/10.1108/00251741011043902.

Amit, Raphael H., and Christoph Zott. "Business Model Innovation: Creating Value in Times of Change." *IESE Business School Working Paper*, No. 870 (July 2010): doi.org/10.2139/ssrn.1701660.

Antoncic, Bostjan, and Robert D. Hisrich. "Clarifying the Intrapreneurship Concept." *Journal of Small Business and Enterprise Development* 10, No. 1 (2003): 7–24, doi.org/10.1108/14626000310461187.

Anu, L., "Fostering Intrapreneurship: The New Competitive Edge." Indian Institute of Management Kozhikode, May 2007.

Benitez-Amado, Jose, Francisco Javier Llorens-Montes, and Maria Nieves Perez-Arostegui. "Information Technology-enabled

Intrapreneurship Culture and Firm Performance." Industrial Management & Data Systems 110, No. 4 (2010): 550–66, doi.org/10.1108/02635571011039025.

Berfield, Susan, Eliza Ronalds-Hannon, Matthew Townsend, and Lauren Coleman-Lochner. "Tears 'R' Us: The World's Biggest Toy Store Didn't Have to Die." Bloomberg Business Week, June 6, 2018, bloomberg.com/news/features/2018-06-06/toys-r-us-the-world-s-biggest-toy-store-didn-t-have-to-die.

Blumenthal, Neil. "Warby Parker CEO: The One Thing We Ask Employees to Do Every Week." *Fortune*. Published March 6, 2017, fortune.com/2017/03/06/warby-parker-ceo-neil-blumenthal-innovation-creativity/.

Chetty, Sylvie, and Colin Campbell-Hunt. "A Strategic Approach to Internationalization: A Traditional Versus a 'Born-Global' Approach." *Journal of International Marketing* 12, No. 1 (2004): 57–81, doi.org/10.1509/jimk.12.1.57.25651.

Cresswell, John, and Cheryl Poth. *Qualitative Inquiry and Research Design*, No. 4. London: Sage Publications, 2013.

Dottore, Antonio, and David Corkindale. "Towards a Theory of Business Model Adaptation." Swinburne, 2009.

Dweck, C. S. *Mindset: The New Psychology of Success*. New York: Random House, 2006.

Edvinsson, Leif, and Michael S. Malone. *Intellectual Capital: The Proven Way to Establish Your Company's True Value by Measuring Its Hidden Brainpower*. New York: Piatkus Books, 1997.

Eesley, Dale T., and Clinton O. Longenecker. "Gateways to Intrapreneurship." *Industrial Management* 48, No. 1 (2006).

Engels, Coert. "We Are Born Creative Geniuses and the Education System Dumbs Us Down, According to NASA Scientists." Ideapod. Published December 16, 2017, ideapod.com/born-creative-geniuses-education-system-dumbs-us-according-nasa-scientists/.

Ferdows, Kasra, Michael A. Lewis, and Jose A.D. Machuca. "Zara's Secret for Fast Fashion." Business Research for Business Leaders, Harvard Business School Working Knowledge. Published February 21, 2005, hbswk.hbs.edu/archive/zara-s-secret-for-fast-fashion.

Gino, Francesca. "Let Your Workers Rebel," *Harvard Business Review* (online). Published October 24, 2016, hbr.org/cover-story/2016/10/let-your-workers-rebel.

Gray, David E., *Doing Research in the Real World*. London: Sage Publications, 2009.

Gringarten, Hagai, Lisa J. Knowles, Raúl Fernández-Calienes, and Nicole Grandmont-Gariboldi. "The Branding of an Academic Journal: How Marketing, Intrapreneurship, Information Technology, and Teamwork Created a Successful Research Journal." *Journal of Multidisciplinary Research* 3, No. 3 (2011): 109–23.

Gumbe, Samuel M. "Intrapreneurship as an Alternative Strategy to Firms' Competitiveness: The Case of Harare Based Manufacturers." *International Journal of Physical and Social Sciences* 5, No. 8 (August 2015): 77–105.

Ireland, R. Duane, Jeffrey G. Covin, and Donald F. Kuratko. "Conceptualizing Corporate Entrepreneurship Strategy." *Entrepreneurship Theory and Practice* 33, No. 1 (2008): 19–46.

Jelenc, Lara, John Pisapia, and Natalija Ivanušić. "Demographic Variables Influencing Individual Entrepreneurial Orientation and Strategic Thinking Capability." *Journal of Economic and Social Development* 3, No. 1 (2016): papers.ssrn.com/sol3/papers.cfm?abstract_id=2715121.

Johnson, Phil, and Joanne Duberley. *Understanding Management Research*. London: Sage Publications, 2000.

Kawasaki, Guy. "Reality Check: The Irreverent Guide to Outsmarting, Outmanaging, and Outmarketing Your Competition." *Strategic Direction* 26, No. 11 (2010): doi.org/10.1108/sd.2010.05626kae.002.

Kawasaki, G. "How to Change the World: The Art of Intrapreneurship." Published January 4, 2016, guykawasaki.com/the_art_of_intr/.

Khavul, Susanna, Mark Peterson, Drake Mullens, and Abdul A. Rasheed. "Going Global with Innovations from Emerging Economies: Investment in Customer Support Capabilities Pays Off." *Journal of International Marketing* 18, No. 4 (2013): 22–42, doi.org/10.1509/jimk.18.4.22.

Kotler, Philip, and Kevin Lane Keller. *Marketing Management*. Upper Saddle River, N.J.: Pearson Prentice Hall, 2009.

Kotter, John P. "Leading Change." *Harvard Business Review*, January 2007.

Krantz, David. "The CEO of YP on Leading Digital Transformation." Interview by Sarah Green. *Harvard Business Review*, July 23, 2015. Audio, 21:28. hbr.org/ideacast/2015/07/the-ceo-of-yp-on-leading-digital-transformation.html.

Kuratko, Donald F., Jeffrey S. Hornsby, and James Hayton. "Corporate Entrepreneurship: The Innovative Challenge for a New Global Economic Reality." *Small Business Economics* 45, No. 2 (January 2015): 245–53.

Kvale, Steinar, and Svend Brinkmann. *InterViews: Learning the Craft of Qualitative Research Interviewing*. London: Sage Publications, 2009.

Liping, Wang, Jiang Jie, Lee Naiqiu, and Xu Zhengzhong. "The Research on the Dynamic Management Mechanisms of Product Innovation Intrapreneurship of SMEs." *2010 IEEE International Conference on Advanced Management Science* 3 (July 2010): 617–21.

Magnusson, Niklas. "H&M Closing Most Stores in Two Decades." *Bloomberg*, January 31, 2018, bloomberg.com/news/articles/2018-10-22/wall-street-s-lacrosse-fraternity-backs-rabil-s-upstart-league.

Mayring, Phillipp. "On Generalization in Qualitatively Oriented Research." *Forum: Qualitative Social Research* 8, No. 3, Art. 26 (2007): nbn-resolving.de/urn:nbn:de:0114-fqs0703262.

McLeod, Saul. "Asch Experiment." *Simply Psychology*. Published 2008, simplypsychology.org/asch-conformity.html.

Molina, Carlos, and Jamie L. Callahan. "Fostering Organizational Performance: The Role of Learning and Intrapreneurship." *Journal of European Industrial Training* 33, No. 5 (2009): 388–400, doi.org/10.1108/03090590910966553.

Nason, Robert S., Alexander McKelvie, and G.T. Lumpkin. "The Role of Organizational Size in the Heterogeneous Nature of Corporate Entrepreneurship." *Small Business Economics* 45, No. 2 (2015): 279–304, doi.org/10.1007/s11187-015-9632-6.

Orr, H. Allen. "The Genetic Theory of Adaptation: A Brief History." *Nature Reviews Genetics* 6 (February 2005): 119–27, doi.org/10.1038/nrg1523.

Oshin, Mayo. "Elon Musk's '3-Step' First Principles Thinking: How to Think and Solve Difficult Problems Like a Genius." mayooshin.com/first-principles-thinking.

Parker, Simon C. "Intrapreneurship or Entrepreneurship?" *Journal of Business Venturing* 26, No. 1 (2011): 19–34, doi.org/10.1016/j.jbusvent.2009.07.003.

Pinchot III, Gifford. "Intrapreneuring: Why You Don't Have to Leave the Corporation to Become an Entrepreneur." *Urbana-Champaign's Academy for Entrepreneurial Leadership Historical Research Reference in Entrepreneurship*, University of Illinois: papers.ssrn.com/sol3/papers.cfm?abstract_id=1496196.

Punch, Keith. *Introduction to Social Research: Quantitative and Qualitative Approaches*. London: Sage Publications, 2005.

Reiter, Raymond. "A Theory of Diagnosis From First Principles." *Artificial Intelligence* 32, No. 1 (April 1987): 57–95, doi.org/10.1016/0004-3702(87)90062-2.

Sbordone, Argia M., Jordi Gali, and Mark Gertler. "Globalization and Inflation Dynamics: The Impact of Increased Competition." *National Bureau of Economic Research*, 2009.

Snyder, Mark, and Nancy Cantor. "Testing Hypotheses About Other People: The Use of Historical Knowledge." *Journal of Experimental Social Psychology* 15, No. 4 (July 1979): 330–42, doi.org/10.1016/0022-1031(79)90042-8.

Steiber, Annika, and Sverker Alänge. "A Corporate System for Continuous Innovation: The Case of Google Inc." *European Journal of Innovation Management* 12, No. 2 (2013): 243–64, doi.org/10.1108/14601061311324566.

"The E-mail Larry Page Should Have Written to James Damore." *The Economist*, August 19, 2017, economist.com/international/2017/08/19/the-e-mail-larry-page-should-have-written-to-james-damore.

Wilson, David Sloan. *Evolution for Everyone: How Darwin's Theory Can Change the Way We Think About Our Lives*. New York: Delacorte Press, 2007.

Wymbs, Cliff. "How E-commerce Is Transforming and Internationalizing Service Industries." *Journal of Services Marketing* 14, No. 6 (2000): 463–77, doi.org/10.1108/08876040010347598.

Zheng, Shihui. "The Failure of Home Depot in China — A Case Study." Red Fame, *Business and Management Studies* 3, No. 4 (December 2017): doi.org/10.11114/bms.v3i4.2791.

# INDEX

*Cherished Fortune: Make Your Wealth Your Business*
Andrew Allentuck and Benoit Poliquin

**How new investors can start using a small-business mindset to maximize their wealth.**

An early start in investing can be a huge advantage, but investors must quickly learn to make the most of opportunities. Thinking like a small-business owner can yield great benefits to investors' portfolios. Running a small business means selling goods you know inside and out to customers you know equally well: what they like, what they buy, what they reject.

Using a similar mindset, novice investors can manage their portfolios by understanding what works, controlling risk, and building knowledge. It's about knowing the details of what is in their portfolio and how each stock, and the company behind it, operates. Columnist Andrew Allentuck and financial planner Benoit Poliquin give new investors a much-needed introduction to the critical skills that will maximize their investments' values over their lifetimes.

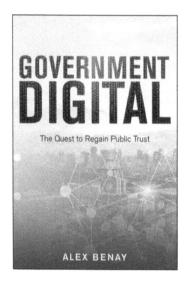

*Government Digital:*
*The Quest to Regain Public Trust*
Alex Benay

**Governments all over the world are consistently outpaced by digital change, and are falling behind.**

Digital government is a better performing government. It is better at providing services people and businesses need. Receiving benefits, accessing health records, registering companies, applying for licences, voting — all of this can be done online or through digital self-service. Digital technology makes government more efficient, reduces hassle, and lowers costs. But what will it take to make governments digital?

Good governance will take nothing short of a metamorphosis of the public sector. With contributions from industry, academic, and government experts — including Hillary Hartley, chief digital officer for Ontario, and Salim Ismail, founder of Singularity University — *Government Digital* lays down a blueprint for this radical change.

*Throw Your Stuff Off the Plane: Achieving Accountability in Business and Life*
Art Horn

**A guide to making the leap from imposed accountability to personal commitment for both individuals and organizations.**

Accountability — we all want the people around us to be responsible, reveal genuine commitment, keep their word, and stay away from blaming others. But organizational systems that aim to institutionalize accountability don't quite go all the way. People are people. They have their own wants and needs, their own psychological tangles, and they often don't particularly want to be held accountable, let alone confront others who have let them down.

*Throw Your Stuff Off the Plane* is here to help. It reveals the missing ingredient organizations usually overlook: personal responsibility. It's an approach to self-improvement for each reader, centring on untangling the conflicting thoughts that block personal responsibility. And it's a guide for every leader who wants to go all the way.

**Book Credits**
Developmental Editor: Dominic Farrell
Project Editor: Elena Radic
Copy Editor: Jonathan Schmidt
Proofreader: Megan Beadle
Indexer: Sergey Lobachev

Designer: Laura Boyle

Publicist: Elham Ali

**Dundurn**
Publisher: J. Kirk Howard
Vice-President: Carl A. Brand
Editorial Director: Kathryn Lane
Artistic Director: Laura Boyle
Production Manager: Rudi Garcia
Director of Sales and Marketing: Synora Van Drine
Publicity Manager: Michelle Melski
Manager, Accounting and Technical Services: Livio Copetti

Editorial: Allison Hirst, Dominic Farrell, Jenny McWha, Rachel Spence,
Elena Radic, Melissa Kawaguchi
Marketing and Publicity: Kendra Martin, Kathryn Bassett, Elham Ali,
Tabassum Siddiqui, Heather McLeod
Design and Production: Sophie Paas-Lang

dundurn.com          dundurnpress
@dundurnpress        dundurnpress
dundurnpress         info@dundurn.com

FIND US ON NETGALLEY & GOODREADS TOO!

DUNDURN